MW00592217

OPPOSING
VIEWPOINTS®
SERIES

Whistleblowers

Other Books of Related Interest

Opposing Viewpoints Series

Police Reform
Politics and Journalism in a Post-Truth World
White Collar Crime

At Issue Series

The Ethics of Wikileaks
The Media's Influence on Society
Policing in America

Current Controversies Series

The Dark Web
Freedom of the Press
Whistleblowers

"Congress shall make
no law ... abridging
the freedom of speech,
or of the press."

First Amendment to the U.S. Constitution

The basic foundation of our democracy is the First Amendment guarantee of freedom of expression. The Opposing Viewpoints series is dedicated to the concept of this basic freedom and the idea that it is more important to practice it than to enshrine it.

| Whistleblowers

Gary Wiener, Book Editor

Published in 2023 by Greenhaven Publishing, LLC
2544 Clinton Street,
Buffalo NY 14224

Articles in Greenhaven Publishing anthologies are often edited for length to meet page
requirements. In addition, original titles of these works are changed to clearly present
the main thesis and to explicitly indicate the author's opinion. Every effort is made to
ensure that Greenhaven Publishing accurately reflects the original intent of the authors.
Every effort has been made to trace the owners of the copyrighted material.

Cover image: Reshetnikov_art/Shutterstock.com

Library of Congress CataloginginPublication Data

Names: Wiener, Gary, editor.
Title: Whistleblowers / edited by Gary Wiener.
Description: First Edition. | New York : Greenhaven Publishing, 2024. | Series:
Opposing viewpoints | Includes bibliographic references and index.
Identifiers: ISBN 9781534509375 (pbk.) | ISBN 9781534509382 (library bound)
Subjects: LCSH: Whistle blowing--Juvenile literature. | Corruption--Prevention--Juvenile
literature. | Crime prevention--Juvenile literature. | Ethics--Juvenile literature.
Classification: LCC HD60.W485 2024 | DDC 342.73'068--dc23

Manufactured in the United States of America

Website: http://greenhavenpublishing.com

Contents

Chapter 3: Should Police Officers Break the Code of Silence and Blow the Whistle?

Chapter 4: Are Government Whistleblowers Heroes or Traitors?

The Importance of Opposing Viewpoints

Perhaps every generation experiences a period in time in which the populace seems especially polarized, starkly divided on the important issues of the day and gravitating toward the far ends of the political spectrum and away from a consensus-facilitating middle ground. The world that today's students are growing up in and that they will soon enter into as active and engaged citizens is deeply fragmented in just this way. Issues relating to terrorism, immigration, women's rights, minority rights, race relations, health care, taxation, wealth and poverty, the environment, policing, military intervention, the proper role of government—in some ways, perennial issues that are freshly and uniquely urgent and vital with each new generation—are currently roiling the world.

If we are to foster a knowledgeable, responsible, active, and engaged citizenry among today's youth, we must provide them with the intellectual, interpretive, and critical-thinking tools and experience necessary to make sense of the world around them and of the all-important debates and arguments that inform it. After all, the outcome of these debates will in large measure determine the future course, prospects, and outcomes of the world and its peoples, particularly its youth. If they are to become successful members of society and productive and informed citizens, students need to learn how to evaluate the strengths and weaknesses of someone else's arguments, how to sift fact from opinion and fallacy, and how to test the relative merits and validity of their own opinions against the known facts and the best possible available information. The landmark series Opposing Viewpoints has been providing students with just such critical-thinking skills and exposure to the debates surrounding society's most urgent contemporary issues for many years, and it continues to serve this essential role with undiminished commitment, care, and rigor.

The key to the series's success in achieving its goal of sharpening students' critical-thinking and analytic skills resides in its title—

Opposing Viewpoints. In every intriguing, compelling, and engaging volume of this series, readers are presented with the widest possible spectrum of distinct viewpoints, expert opinions, and informed argumentation and commentary, supplied by some of today's leading academics, thinkers, analysts, politicians, policy makers, economists, activists, change agents, and advocates. Every opinion and argument anthologized here is presented objectively and accorded respect. There is no editorializing in any introductory text or in the arrangement and order of the pieces. No piece is included as a "straw man," an easy ideological target for cheap point-scoring. As wide and inclusive a range of viewpoints as possible is offered, with no privileging of one particular political ideology or cultural perspective over another. It is left to each individual reader to evaluate the relative merits of each argument— as he or she sees it, and with the use of ever-growing critical-thinking skills—and grapple with his or her own assumptions, beliefs, and perspectives to determine how convincing or successful any given argument is and how the reader's own stance on the issue may be modified or altered in response to it.

This process is facilitated and supported by volume, chapter, and selection introductions that provide readers with the essential context they need to begin engaging with the spotlighted issues, with the debates surrounding them, and with their own perhaps shifting or nascent opinions on them. In addition, guided reading and discussion questions encourage readers to determine the authors' point of view and purpose, interrogate and analyze the various arguments and their rhetoric and structure, evaluate the arguments' strengths and weaknesses, test their claims against available facts and evidence, judge the validity of the reasoning, and bring into clearer, sharper focus the reader's own beliefs and conclusions and how they may differ from or align with those in the collection or those of their classmates.

Research has shown that reading comprehension skills improve dramatically when students are provided with compelling, intriguing, and relevant "discussable" texts. The subject matter of these collections could not be more compelling, intriguing, or urgently relevant to today's students and the world they are poised to inherit. The anthologized articles and the reading and discussion questions that are included with them also provide the basis for stimulating, lively, and passionate classroom debates. Students who are compelled to anticipate objections to their own argument and identify the flaws in those of an opponent read more carefully, think more critically, and steep themselves in relevant context, facts, and information more thoroughly. In short, using discussable text of the kind provided by every single volume in the Opposing Viewpoints series encourages close reading, facilitates reading comprehension, fosters research, strengthens critical thinking, and greatly enlivens and energizes classroom discussion and participation. The entire learning process is deepened, extended, and strengthened.

For all of these reasons, Opposing Viewpoints continues to be exactly the right resource at exactly the right time—when we most need to provide readers with the critical-thinking tools and skills that will not only serve them well in school but also in their careers and their daily lives as decision-making family members, community members, and citizens. This series encourages respectful engagement with and analysis of opposing viewpoints and fosters a resulting increase in the strength and rigor of one's own opinions and stances. As such, it helps make readers "future ready," and that readiness will pay rich dividends for the readers themselves, for the citizenry, for our society, and for the world at large.

Introduction

*"We live in the age of
the whistleblower."*

-Jordan Thomas,
American attorney

The 2020s have been notable for a number of startling changes. It is an age of infection, as COVID-19, the flu, and diseases of the unvaccinated have filled the headlines. It is the age of the remote worker, as more and more employees are working off-site. And it is the age of the whistleblower. Whereas in the past, government officials, police officers, and corporate executives had often engaged in misconduct with impunity, a new wave of whistleblowers has made those in power think twice about playing the system. "We live in the age of the whistleblower," says Jordan Thomas, a former Securities and Exchange Commission (SEC) official.[1]

Whistleblowers have become so pervasive and powerful in society that even 20 years ago, *Time Magazine* acknowledged three women whistleblowers as *Persons of the Year*. The three were WorldCom employee Cynthia Cooper, Enron executive Sherron Watkins, and Colleen Rowley of the FBI.[2] Watkins was the Enron vice president who wrote to chairman Kenneth Lay in the summer of 2001, warning him that their accounting methods were irregular. In January of the next year during Congressional hearings on Enron, Watkins became a reluctant public figure. According to *Time* Magazine, "the Year of the Whistle-Blower began."[3]

Rowley was an FBI attorney. In May 2001, she sent a memo to then-FBI Director Robert Mueller (later of Mueller Report fame) about how the bureau ignored requests from her field office in Minnesota to investigate terrorist Zacarias Moussaoui, who participated in the 9/11 hijackings.

In June of 2001, Cooper exposed fraudulent accounting practices at WorldCom, a telecommunications company. Using phony bookkeeping, the company had covered up $3.8 billion in losses.

Since that time, all three women have been involved in efforts to clean up corporate behavior. Watkins and Cooper wrote books about their experiences. Rowley ran for public office, though unsuccessfully.

While there have been false claims laws governing corporate practices in the United States dating back to the 19th century, the Enron and WorldCom scandals ushered in a new period of anti-fraud and whistleblower legislation. Nevertheless, there has been no shortage of corrupt and fraudulent behavior in the 21st century, and despite the increase in whistleblowing activity as well as laws to protect such activity, there are few signs that it is being reined in.

In 2002, the Sarbanes–Oxley Act (SOX) was enacted to curb corporate fraud. SOX provided whistleblower protections prohibiting a wide range of retaliatory measures, including firing, demoting, suspending, threatening, harassing, or in any other manner discriminating against a whistleblower.

After the financial crisis of 2008, the U.S. government created legislation to stem fraud and to promote whistleblowing. The Dodd-Frank Act, known formally as the Dodd-Frank Wall Street Reform and Consumer Protection Act, became law in 2010. This major piece of reform legislation covered commodities and securities actions worldwide. The act promoted financial stability by addressing accountability and transparency in the financial system.

The law also addressed whistleblowing. According to the Securities and Exchange Commission website, the Dodd Frank Act

> provides that the Commission shall pay awards to eligible whistleblowers who voluntarily provide the SEC with original information that leads to a successful enforcement action

yielding monetary sanctions of over $1 million. The award amount is required to be between 10 percent and 30 percent of the total monetary sanctions collected in the Commission's action or any related action such as in a criminal case.[4]

In addition, Dodd-Frank

also expressly prohibits retaliation by employers against whistleblowers and provides them with a private cause of action in the event that they are discharged or discriminated against by their employers in violation of the Act.[5]

Similar protections had been installed for government employees by the 1989 Whistleblower Protection Act (WPA), but in 2012, the Congress strengthened these laws by passing the Whistleblower Protection Enhancement Act (WPEA). The WPEA enhanced protections for Federal employees who report fraud, waste, and abuse.

Despite these laws, whistleblowing is still an incredibly dangerous endeavor. In the 20th century, two of the now most famous whistleblowers paid a steep price. Police whistleblower Frank Serpico was likely set up by his own colleagues and shot in the face in 1971 for exposing corruption in the New York Police Department. After the attempted murder, he was awarded a police Medal of Honor, but he also spent the next decade in self-exile in Switzerland, recovering from his ordeal.

Karen Silkwood was a whistleblower who exposed dangerous practices at Kerr-McGee Cimarron Fuel Fabrication Site in Oklahoma, a facility that made plutonium pellets. In 1974, on the way to a meeting with a journalist, her car crashed in mysterious circumstances, and she was killed. Incriminating papers that she carried with her on the front seat of her car were never found.

Numerous famous whistleblowers in the 21st century have had their lives completely disrupted. Unless whistleblowers are strategic or lucky enough to remain anonymous and work through an attorney, they are likely to be fired, forced to resign, or even prosecuted. Edward Snowden, who leaked documents concerning the National Security Agency's surveillance program in 2013, is in exile in Russia. Reality Winner, who exposed the Trump administration's cover up of Russian interference in the 2016 United States elections, ended up serving prison time. Rebekah Jones was fired from the Florida Department of Health in 2020 for claiming that Florida manipulated important COVID-19 data for political purposes. Peter Zatko, former Twitter Chief Security Officer, was allegedly fired in 2022 for refusing to cover up security vulnerabilities. The list goes on and on.

Cases such as these are why professor of law Jonathan Turley has characterized certain whistleblower protections as "a colossal joke."[6] Nonetheless, many argue that whistleblowers play an essential role in holding those in power accountable and preventing immoral, illegal, and sometimes dangerous misdeeds.

Opposing Viewpoints: Whistleblowers presents a wide range of viewpoints that expand upon, clarify, and debate many of the above-mentioned issues. It provides a valuable resource for those readers who want to investigate the complex issues involved in whistleblowing.

Notes

1. "The Age of the Whistleblower," the *Economist*, December 3, 2015. https://www.economist.com/business/2015/12/03/the-age-of-the-whistleblower.
2. "2002: The Whistleblowers," *Time*, March 5, 2020. https://time.com/5793757/the-whistleblowers-100-women-of-the-year/.
3. *Ibid.*
4. Carlo V. di Florio, "Speech by SEC Staff: Keynote Address at the SIFMA Anti-Money Laundering Seminar," U.S. Securities and Exchange Commission, March 3, 2011. https://www.sec.gov/news/speech/2011/spch030311cvd.htm.
5. *Ibid.*
6. Jonathan Turley, "Edward Snowden: Whistleblower or Traitor?" *Al Jazeera*, June 9, 2014. https://www.aljazeera.com/opinions/2014/6/9/edward-snowden-whistleblower-or-traitor.

CHAPTER 1

Do Whistleblower Rewards Work?

Chapter Preface

The traditional whistleblower was an insider, someone with intimate knowledge of the internal workings of a corporation, government organization, or other entity. As an insider, they sensed wrongdoing, and, perhaps having unsuccessfully tried to warn their colleagues, bosses, or executives, turned to a law firm to help them expose the ugly truth.

Those outside an organization who also intuited wrongdoing were often ignored or maligned.

For example, there is the case of whistleblower Harry Markopolos, a former securities firm executive. In 1999, Markopolos' bosses, worried about losing clients to a more successful hedge fund, tasked him with trying to duplicate that fund's earnings. The competing hedge fund was run by Bernie Madoff, former chairman of the Nasdaq Stock Market, whose fund was generating unmatched profits for its clients.[1]

When Markopolos, a "quant" (or quantitative analyst) ran the numbers on Madoff's firm, he immediately knew something was wrong. Though he was an outsider and had no access to the Madoff firm's internal workings, he realized that the hedge fund could not legitimately be yielding such remarkable returns for investors. Markopolos suspected one of two things: that Madoff was running a Ponzi scheme or using insider trading information. Both were illegal.

In 2000, Markopolos took his findings to the Securities and Exchange Commission (SEC), which oversees stock market trading, but was rebuffed. They did not believe an outsider's information was relevant or correct, in part because Madoff was such a monumental figure on the stock trading scene. Markopolos kept trying, alerting the SEC again both in 2001 and 2005, to no avail. A few years later, Madoff's own sons turned him in after their father, worried he could no longer keep up the fraud, revealed the scheme to them. One of Madoff's sons as well as his sister and brother-in-law died by suicide. Madoff himself died in jail. Restitution was made to some of Madoff's clients, but many more suffered catastrophic and crippling financial losses. For example, it is said that Madoff almost destroyed the New York Mets baseball organization, whose owner at the time, Fred Wilpon, had invested heavily in the fraudulent hedge fund.

Vindicated by the Madoff revelations, Markopolos subsequently accused the General Electric Company of fraud and deceit, but was again rebuffed. This time, it seems, his numbers were not correct. Nevertheless, he currently works with attorneys seeking to expose corporate fraud. The difference is that now there are large cash rewards for doing what Markopolos formerly did for free.

As a result of the financial crisis of 2008 and the exposure of Madoff's deceit, in 2010 Congress passed The Dodd–Frank Wall Street Reform and Consumer Protection Act, commonly referred to as Dodd–Frank. Among other things, it authorizes substantial payments to those who expose corporate fraud. In the aftermath of the Madoff case, outsider whistleblowing has become much more accepted. According to the website of the law firm Constantine and Cannon, "Having once ignored outsiders, the SEC is now in court defending their right to blow the whistle. In a recent opinion, Judge Victor Marrero of the Southern District of New York denied a defendant's attempt to place daylight between 'outsider' whistleblowers and those 'in the room.'"[2]

Whether insider or outsider, whistleblowing can be extraordinarily lucrative, though it should be noted that for many whistleblowers, the monetary incentives do not outweigh the risks. Whistleblower rewards, which can entail 10 to 30 percent of any recovered monies from fraudulent corporate activity, now run into the hundreds of millions of dollars or more. With attorneys taking a substantial share of these rewards, it is not surprising that firms are now actively seeking out potential whistleblowers. The term "professional whistleblower" has been recently coined to denote those, such as quantitative analysts like Markopolos, who work with attorneys to expose corporate fraud and garner huge financial rewards.

Some have argued that hundred-million-dollar payouts are excessive, but as long as government agencies are recouping many times that figure from fraudulent corporate activity, whistleblower rewards are likely to keep increasing.

Notes

1. Andrew Clark, "The Man Who Blew the Whistle on Bernie Madoff," the *Guardian*, March 24, 2010. https://www.theguardian.com/business/2010/mar/24/bernard-madoff-whistleblower-harry-markopolos.
2. "Federal Court Confirms That Outsiders Can Be Whistleblowers Too," July 30, 2021. https://constantinecannon.com/whistleblower/whistleblower-insider-blog/outsiders-can-be-sec-whistleblower-too/.

> *"Whistleblower rewards have been extraordinarily effective in strengthening the enforcement of anti-fraud laws and halting fraud schemes."*

The U.S. Government Rewards Whistleblowers

Jason Zuckerman and Matthew Stock

Jason Zuckerman and Matthew Stock provide an overview of the whistleblower system in the United States. They explain that a whistleblower reward is a monetary incentive given by the government to reward a whistleblower's exposing of actions by a corporation or government entity that leads to a successful prosecution. Whistleblower rewards can be extraordinarily high, into the millions of dollars, depending on the value of the information revealed. Such high payments are well worth it when compared to the amount of money the government may gain from prosecuting corrupt entities. Jason Zuckerman is an attorney who litigates whistleblower retaliation, whistleblower rewards, wrongful discharge, and other employment-related claims. Matthew Stock is the Director of the Whistleblower Rewards Practice at Zuckerman Law.

As you read, consider the following questions:

"What is a whistleblower reward?" by Jason Zuckerman and Matthew Stock, Zuckerman Law, September 21, 2022. Reprinted by permission.

1. What is the highest payment given to a whistleblower, according to the viewpoint?
2. What is a "*qui tam*" lawsuit?
3. What are some of the ways that the government protects whistleblowers?

A whistleblower reward is a monetary incentive provided by the government to reward a whistleblower's disclosure of original information that leads to successful enforcement action. Some whistleblower rewards laws permit whistleblowers to report fraud anonymously and most whistleblower reward laws protect whistleblowers against retaliation. A whistleblower can receive an award of up to 30% of the monetary sanctions collected in a successful enforcement action.

Whistleblower rewards have been extraordinarily effective in strengthening the enforcement of anti-fraud laws and halting fraud schemes. Our clients' SEC whistleblower tips have helped the SEC halt more than $1 billion in fraudulent investment schemes.

Experienced and effective whistleblower rewards lawyers can help you determine if you qualify for a whistleblower reward and work with you to maximize your recovery under various whistleblower reward programs, including the following:

- SEC Whistleblower Reward Program: whistleblower rewards for reporting violations of the federal securities laws. The largest SEC whistleblower reward to date is $114 million.
- Commodity Futures Trading Commission (CFTC) Whistleblower Reward Program: whistleblower rewards for reporting violations of the Commodity Exchange Act. The largest CFTC whistleblower reward to date is $200 million.
- Internal Revenue Service (IRS) Whistleblower Reward Program: whistleblower rewards for reporting tax fraud or underpayments. The largest IRS whistleblower reward to date is $104 million.

- False Claims Act / Qui Tam Lawsuits: whistleblower rewards for reporting fraud on the government. The largest qui tam whistleblower reward to date is $250 million.
- Anti-Money Laundering Whistleblower Reward Program: whistleblower rewards for reporting money laundering.

Each whistleblower program has unique rules and procedures. Whistleblowers should consult with an experienced whistleblower rewards law firm to determine if their claim qualifies for a reward under one of these programs.

SEC Whistleblower Reward Program

Under the SEC Whistleblower Reward Program, the SEC will issue awards to whistleblowers who provide original information that leads to enforcement actions with total monetary sanctions (penalties, disgorgement, and interest) in excess of $1 million. A whistleblower may receive an award of between 10% to 30% of the monetary sanctions collected.

Since 2012, the SEC has issued more than $1 billion in awards to whistleblowers. The largest SEC whistleblower awards to date are $114 million and $110 million.

The program allows whistleblowers to submit anonymous tips to the SEC if represented by an attorney. Whistleblowers are also afforded substantial protection against retaliation.

The most common tips to the SEC Office of the Whistleblower involve:

- Accounting fraud;
- Investment and securities fraud;
- Insider trading;
- Foreign bribery and other FCPA violations;
- EB-5 investment fraud;
- Manipulation of a security's price or volume;
- Fraudulent securities offerings and Ponzi schemes;
- Hedge fund fraud;
- Unregistered securities offerings;

- Investment adviser fraud;
- Broker-dealer anti-money laundering program violations;
- False or misleading statements about a company or investment;
- Inadequate internal controls;
- Deceptive non-generally accepted accounting principles (GAAP) financials;
- Improper revenue recognition;
- Violations of auditor independence rules;
- Misleading or incomplete cybersecurity disclosures; and
- Blockchain and cryptocurrency fraud.

CFTC Whistleblower Reward Program

Under the CFTC Whistleblower Reward Program, the CFTC will issue awards to whistleblowers who provide original information about violations of the Commodity Exchange Act that leads to enforcement actions with total monetary sanctions in excess of $1 million. A whistleblower may receive an award of between 10% to 30% of the monetary sanctions collected. Recently, the CFTC awarded $200 million to a whistleblower.

The program allows whistleblowers to submit anonymous tips to the CFTC if represented by an attorney. Whistleblowers are also afforded substantial protection against retaliation.

IRS Whistleblower Reward Program

Under the IRS Whistleblower Reward Program, the IRS provides whistleblower rewards to individuals of 15% to 30% of proceeds collected from tax fraud or tax underpayments if:

- the whistleblower provides a tip that the IRS decides to take action on (a whistleblower cannot force the IRS to act on a tip);
- the amount in dispute (the tax underpayment, including interest and penalties) exceeds $2 million (if the taxpayer is an individual, his or her gross income must exceed $200,000 for at least one of the tax years in question); and

- the IRS collects tax underpayments resulting from the action (including any related actions).
- The largest IRS whistleblower reward to date is $104 million, which was issued to Bradley Birkenfeld after he blew the whistle on UBS for helping wealthy Americans hide their assets and evade taxes.

False Claims Act/Qui Tam Whistleblower Law

The False Claims Act contains a qui tam whistleblower rewards provision allowing whistleblowers, or qui tam "relators," to bring suits on behalf of the United States against wrongdoers who are defrauding the government. Whistleblowers are eligible to receive 15% to 30% of monetary recoveries. Whistleblowers are also afforded substantial protection against retaliation under the Act.

Qui tam actions brought by whistleblowers have enabled the Department of Justice has to recover nearly $70 billion in stolen government funds, and whistleblowers initiate nearly 80 percent of False Claims Act recoveries.

THE PROS AND CONS OF FILING A FALSE CLAIMS ACT

The federal False Claims Act, a.k.a. the "Lincoln Law," was enacted by Congress in 1863. The purpose of the Act was to prevent, and provide legal recourse for fraud during the Civil War. At the time, war-profiteers were exploiting the armies of the North and the South. Selling faulty weaponry, rancid rations, and sick and decrepit horses and mules.

The Lincoln Law set forth a provision that allowed the whistleblower to receive a reward known as "qui tam." In 1986 the False Claims Act was amended, a new provision increased the qui tam plaintiff's reward to 15% to 30% per false claim. For example, the whistleblowers in the recent Cephalon drug case split $46.4 million four ways. Quite a payday by any standard, even on Wall Street!

A liable defendant will be imposed with treble damages and civil fines of $5,000 to $10,000 per false claim. All elements of a claim under the False Claims Act are held up to a preponderance of the evidence standard. Simply put, whether the defendant more likely than not submitted false claims.

Blowing the whistle on your employer is not something that is easy to do, nor should it be taken lightly. Jeffrey Wigand, arguably the most famous whistleblower, endured harassment and death threats for exposing the Big Tobacco practice of "impact boosting." Ultimately, Jeffrey got his story out on *60 Minutes* and in the film *The Insider.*

Although it is a tough to blow the whistle on an employer, the False Claims Act provides the necessary amount of compensation for taking such a difficult step. It is good to know that, in this case, the government is on your side.

"Whistleblowing Part II: The Pros and Cons Of Filing A False Claims Act," by David Mittleman, The Legal Examiner, October 5, 2008.

Anti-Retaliation Laws Protecting Whistleblowers

Whistleblowers disclosing fraud to the government or to their employers are protected against retaliation under federal and state laws, including the following:

- Sarbanes-Oxley Act (protecting whistleblower disclosures about violations of SEC rules and regulations; violations of federal laws related to fraud against shareholders; or mail, wire, bank, or securities fraud). Download our free ebook, Sarbanes-Oxley Whistleblower Protection: Robust Protection for Corporate Whistleblowers.
- Taxpayer First Act (protecting whistleblowing about tax fraud or tax underpayment)
- Dodd-Frank Act (protecting whistleblowing to the SEC and CFTC)
- False Claims Act and National Defense Authorization Act (NDAA) (protecting federal contractors)
- Consumer Financial Protection Act (protecting disclosures concerning consumer financial protection)

> "After the effectiveness of
> whistleblowers in rooting out waste,
> fraud, and abuse has repeatedly been
> demonstrated, stronger whistleblower
> laws and incentives are now
> appearing around the world."

Whistleblowing Works Around the Globe

National Whistleblower Center

In this viewpoint, the authors maintain that whistleblowing is a crucial and effective way to root out fraud. They observe that whistleblower laws, including the granting of substantial rewards, are being enacted worldwide. When whistleblowers are protected and offered substantial rewards, their effectiveness is enhanced. The United States has a long history of creating whistleblower laws, and, as such, is a global leader in this area. According to the viewpoint, whistleblower laws have been a powerful deterrent to those contemplating criminal activity. The National Whistleblower Center (NWC) is a leading nonprofit dedicated to protecting and rewarding whistleblowers around the world. They assist whistleblowers in finding legal aid, advocate for stronger whistleblower protection laws, and educate the public about whistleblowers' critical role in protecting democracy and the rule of law.

As you read, consider the following questions:

1. How is whistleblower law continuing to expand on a global scale?
2. How have whistleblower laws in countries such as South Korea and Canada been successful?
3. How do whistleblower laws deter government and corporate criminal activity?

Whistleblowers are the first line of defense against corruption, fraud, and wrongdoing and the single most effective source for information about fraud and other illegal activities. Despite the risk to their professional and personal lives, company insiders, government employees, and others with original information about illegal activity regularly come forward to report crimes that would otherwise go undetected.

Oftentimes the first to discover and report instances of fraud, whistleblowers have proven themselves to be invaluable in the detection of crime and enforcement of various laws. In a 2007 study conducted by PricewaterhouseCoopers, it was found that professional auditors only detected 19% of fraudulent activities at private corporations, while whistleblowers detected and exposed 43%. According to the study, surveyed executives "estimated that the whistleblowers saved their shareholders billions of dollars."

A 2006 study from the University of Chicago Booth School of Business, *Who Blows the Whistle on Corporate Fraud?*, comes to the same conclusion, stating: employees "clearly have the best access to information. Few, if any, fraud can be committed without the knowledge and often the support of several of them. Some might be accomplices…but most are not."

However, in order to ensure that whistleblowers do step forward with evidence of wrongdoing, a robust legal framework of protections and incentives is crucial. After the effectiveness of whistleblowers in rooting out waste, fraud, and abuse has repeatedly been demonstrated, stronger whistleblower laws and incentives are now appearing around the world. As of 2020, whistleblower protection laws have been enacted in at least 59 countries, as well as the United States. However, protections vary from country to country and are not created the same. Many of these laws contain one or two key elements of successful whistleblower laws, but few contain all the elements needed to properly incentivize whistleblower disclosures and protect whistleblowers from retaliation.

As the global expansion of whistleblower protections continues, it's crucial that new laws incorporate and existing laws are updated to include all the key features of successful whistleblowing regimes, including confidentiality, rewards, and the option to report to an independent channel like a government whistleblower office. When whistleblowers have their identities protected and rewards are in place, they are incentivized to step forward and are able to effectively, and safely, blow the whistle through legitimate channels of reporting. The data bears this out: reward laws have been shown to be extremely effective in generating high quality tips that result in successful prosecutions. Examples of successful whistleblower programs include those in the United States and South Korea.

The United States is a leading influence in the global promulgation of these key whistleblower protections, stemming from its long history of whistleblower law. Not only are U.S. whistleblower protection laws among the strongest in the world, many of these laws can be applied transnationally, allowing whistleblowers around the world, U.S. citizens or not, to confidentially report fraud to U.S. law enforcement authorities, as long as the crime has a U.S. nexus.

In the United States, these provisions are enshrined in laws like the False Claims Act, which has a qui tam provision that allows individuals to sue on behalf of the government, and the Dodd-Frank Act, which created whistleblower programs at the Securities and Exchange Commission (SEC) and the Commodity Futures Trading Commission (CFTC) and strengthened the Foreign Corrupt Practices Act (FCPA), an important anti-bribery law.

These laws are proven to recover significant monies for the government and allow whistleblowers to come forward and expose wrongdoing. In Fiscal Year 2020 alone, whistleblower-initiated cases brought in over $1.6 billion in False Claims Act settlements and judgements recovered by the government. Since the Dodd-Frank Act passed in 2010, the SEC and CFTC have recovered over $2.8 billion with more than $840 million being awarded to whistleblowers who assisted in the cases, and under the Foreign Corrupt Practices Act, the U.S. government has collected more than $7.2 billion in FCPA violations. The numbers and vast amount of recoveries stemming from whistleblowers' disclosures speaks to the power of whistleblowing.

U.S. officials and agencies have confirmed the importance of whistleblowers to successful enforcement efforts. The former Chair of the U.S. Securities and Exchange Commission (SEC), Mary Jo White, has said that whistleblowers provide an "invaluable public service, and they should be supported," while noting that the SEC sees itself as "the whistleblower's advocate." White's comments came after the widespread success of the SEC whistleblower program, established in 2011, which as of 2020 has received over 33,300 whistleblower tips from more than 130 countries. Other agencies that have similarly praised the contributions of whistleblowers include the U.S. Justice Department and the U.S. Fish and Wildlife Service.

Similar laws in South Korea and Canada have also shown tremendous success. Through South Korea's whistleblower channel created by the Anti-Corruption and Civil Rights Commission (ACRC) in 2008, whistleblowers have assisted the South Korean government with USD $265 million in recoveries. And in Canada, which offers rewards to individuals who provide information related to "international tax evasion" and "aggressive tax avoidance", whistleblowers in Canada helped the government collect USD $19 million in 2018 to 2019 fiscal year—the first year that awards were issued—alone.

Crucially, these laws also have a deterrent effect on wrongdoers. In a 2014 article in the Villanova Law Review, University of California-Davis professor of law and Chairman of the IRS Advisory Council Dr. Dennis J. Ventry explained that whistleblower disclosures have a major deterrent effect on corporate crime. In the article, Professor Ventry outlined the deterrent effect of whistleblowing: "Whistleblowers can do more than just uncover and report knowing violations of the law. They can also prevent noncompliance from happening in the first place. An effective whistleblower program…would add significant risk to noncompliance by increasing the probability of detection and the likelihood of potential penalties, the two most important variables in traditional tax deterrence models. In turn, increased aversion to noncompliance—due to increased fear of detection and palpable penalties as well as additional variables such as moral, ethical and reputational inputs—would result in increased revenue collection."

To further document the powerful deterrent effect of whistleblowing, Professor Ventry surveyed the literature on crime deterrence and noted that objective, scholarly, and empirical studies had long documented the fact that the "degree of deterrence" of crimes can be "calculated as product of probability of detection." Or, as first explained by the Nobel Prize winning economist Gary S. Becker, "for the individual to elect to engage in crime, the gain relative to its loss must exceed the odds of capture."

In short, whistleblowing works. Stories like that of Howard Wilkinson, Bradley Birkenfeld and Sherron Watkins are testaments to the impact that whistleblowers can have.

Wilkinson, relying on U.S. law, confidentially raised concerns of a $234 billion-dollar illegal money laundering scheme through Danske Bank's Estonia branch. Now European authorities as well as the SEC, IRS and U.S. Justice Department are investigating the scandal and the CEO has resigned.

Birkenfeld's disclosures of illegal offshore Swiss UBS bank accounts held by U.S. citizens helped recover millions for U.S. taxpayers in fines and penalties, and over $5 billion in collections from those who held the illegal accounts. Birkenfeld's efforts culminated in the Swiss government changing its tax treaty with the United States.

And Watkins exposed corporate misconduct at Enron by pointing out accounting irregularities, contributing to the end of a company once considered to be a titan of industry.

In coming forward, despite great personal risks, all of these whistleblowers changed the world.

> "High rewards can motivate potential whistleblowers to come forward because the monetary amount may mitigate the cost of professional and social sanctions that can result."

Whistleblower Payments Are Well Worth the Expenditure

Stephen M. Kohn

In this viewpoint, Stephen M. Kohn remarks on the American government's intent to possibly cap whistleblower awards. Recent multimillion dollar payments to whistleblowers have sparked controversy and conversation that has led to the potential cap. But Kohn argues that large awards are necessary to encourage whistleblowers to risk their careers by informing on corrupt organizations. Kohn describes how recent whistleblowing activity has been well worth the large awards because the result of whistleblower activity is that it often saves far more money than the whistleblower receives, which is only 10 to 30 percent of the corrupt gains. Moreover, successful whistleblowing serves as a deterrent to those contemplating similar crimes. Stephen M. Kohn is a whistleblower lawyer and partner in the qui tam *law firm of Kohn, Kohn and Colapinto and the Chairman of the Board of Directors of the National Whistleblower Center.*

Kohn, Stephen M. "Should Whistleblower Reward Laws Be Capped?" ProMarket, 30 Aug, 2020. Reprinted by permission.

As you read, consider the following questions:

1. How has the Dodd-Frank whistleblower law been a resounding success, according to Kohn?
2. What empirical evidence suggests that whistleblowing acts as a strong deterrent to future financial criminals?
3. According to Kohn, what is the "win-win-win-win" scenario created by whistleblowers.

In 2018, the U.S. Securities and Exchange Commission proposed new rules to its Dodd-Frank Act whistleblower program that could limit the amount of awards paid to whistleblowers in large cases. After two years of consideration, the SEC is posed to finalize its rule on capping the amount of whistleblower rewards. A final vote on the proposed whistleblower rule has been set for September 2nd.

The SEC's proposal to place limits on the size of awards sparked a widespread debate. Under the Dodd-Frank Act, the Commission is required to pay qualified whistleblowers between 10-30% of any sanction obtained from a fraudster. Thus, the SEC could not approve a "hard" cap setting an upward ceiling on the amount of an award. Instead, the SEC proposed a percentage-based cap. Under this "soft" cap, if the SEC obtained over $300 million in sanctions from a fraudster, the whistleblower whose information triggered the enforcement action would be presumptively limited to the lowest percentage award (i.e., a 10 percent recovery).

Over 100,000 public comments were filed in opposition to any cap. Senator Charles Grassley (R-IA), the most respected expert on whistleblowing in Congress, strongly opposed the rule-change. Quoting from the findings of the SEC's Inspector General, Senator Grassley explained: "high rewards can motivate potential whistleblowers to come forward because the monetary amount may mitigate the cost of professional and social sanctions that can result." Numerous whistleblower and investor advocacy groups, along with nationally recognized corporate whistleblowers such as Sherron Watkins (who exposed Enron's fraudulent accounting practices) and Harry Markopolos (who tried to alert the SEC about Bernie Madoff's Ponzi scheme) filed comments strongly opposing the cap. The U.S. Chamber of Commerce supported the cap.

In response to the widespread public opposition, SEC chairman Jay Clayton made clear that the SEC could not set a hard-cap on awards or set any strict monetary limitations. He also expressed concern over how any rule limiting the amount of an award "could deter potential whistleblowers from coming forward."

Moreover, last month, the SEC's Office of the Whistleblower issued a public statement explaining that the Dodd-Frank Act's whistleblower law was extremely successful, resulting in over $2.5 billion in collected sanctions from fraudsters, $750 million returned to "harmed investors," and over $500 million paid in rewards to whistleblowers. Despite these comments, the SEC did not withdraw its proposal to institute a soft percentage-based cap, nor did the SEC indicate how it would resolve the controversy surrounding the proposed rule.

Although the SEC has not yet issued a final rule, mandatory caps have long been supported by organizations that historically opposed whistleblower laws, such as the U.S. Chamber of Commerce. Hard monetary caps are also popular outside the United States, including reward laws enacted in Canada and South Korea.

Weighing the Deterrent Effect When Setting Awards

Larger whistleblower rewards can play very important functions in policing markets and ensuring fair competition. While their ability to incentivize employees to report wrongdoing has long been recognized, the impact that reward-based whistleblowers have on corporate behavior is less well known, but ultimately significantly more far-reaching. Effective reward-based laws have a deterrent effect on criminal activity.

In passing the Dodd-Frank Act, Congress recognized this potential. The Act itself requires the SEC to take "the programmatic interest of the Commission in deterring violations of the securities laws by making awards to whistleblowers who provide information that lead to the successful enforcement of such laws." [emphasis added]. Congress understood that giving awards to whistleblowers could send a very loud message to the market, far beyond simply rewarding a valuable informant for providing excellent information in a timely manner.

The deterrent effect of paying whistleblower rewards is well-documented. In a 2014 article in the Villanova Law Review, University of California-Davis professor of law and Chairman of the IRS Advisory Council, Dennis J. Ventry, explained this effect:

> "Whistleblowers can do more than just uncover and report knowing violations of the law. They can also prevent noncompliance from happening in the first place. An effective whistleblower program . . . would add significant risk to noncompliance by increasing the probability of detection and the likelihood of potential penalties, the two most important variables in traditional tax deterrence models."

Ventry, citing well-documented examples, explained the importance of paying large rewards to increase to public perception that whistleblowers increase the "odds of capture." His conclusion on this matter was clear: "[K]eep whistleblower awards sufficiently high," as "sufficiently high awards" can be used to "induce external reporting of otherwise meritorious claims and provide incentives for whistleblowers to incur the risks and costs associated" with blowing the whistle. Numerous studies fully support Ventry's conclusions. For example, a paper published by the Stockholm School of Economics again confirmed the deterrent effect of paying whistleblower rewards:

> "As for empirical evidence on deterrence, Johannesen and Stolper (2017) found that whistleblowing had deterrence effects in the off-shore banking sector… Wilde (2017) also provides evidence that whistleblowing deters financial misreporting and tax aggressiveness…
>
> …Bigoni et al. (2012) conducted laboratory experiments on leniency policies and rewards as tools to fight cartel formation.

They found that rewards financed by the fines imposed on the other cartel participants had a strong effect on average price (returning it to a competitive level). In the model setting, this implies that rewards have a deterring and desisting effect on cartel formation. The authors also take it that the results are significant for real world scenarios. They also found that cartel formation was significantly lower in a reward environment than in a leniency environment alone."

A study conducted by Philip Berger and Heemin Lee, professors at the University of Chicago Booth School of Business and the Zicklin School of Business at the City University of New York, found that there is "a high direct deterrence value of whistleblower cases." Like Ventry, Berger and Lee recognized the benefits of paying large rewards, finding that the "opportunity for a large payout creates incentives for a whistleblower to come forward with their private information about fraud or misconduct, which can alleviate personal and professional costs arising from whistleblowing on one's employer" and "creates a profit motive for rooting out impropriety."

Jetson Leder-Luis's careful 2019 study Whistleblowers, The False Claims Act, and the Behavior of Healthcare Providers showed that the deterrent value of whistleblower cases is over six-times as great as the immediate enforcement value. Leder-Luis looked at four major health care enforcement actions filed under the qui tam provisions of the False Claims Act. The cases directly resulted in a total of $1.9 billion in government recoveries. However, the deterrent value of these cases over the next five years was calculated to be $18.9 billion. As reported by Leder-Luis:

> "These four whistleblower case studies recovered around $1.9 billion for the federal government, but exhibit even greater benefit in deterrence effects, totaling around $18.9 billion. The average deterrence effect for these cases is around 6.7 times the settlement value over 5 years.
>
> Overall, these results indicate that the direct deterrence benefits of whistleblowing cases often exceed the settlement values many times over, and greatly exceed the retrospective damages used to compute those settlement values. This indicates a large

savings to the Medicare program as a result of these whistleblowing cases, exceeding both the direct recoveries to the government from the settlement as well as the whistleblower compensation.

In addition to the fiscal effects described in the previous section, whistleblowing under the False Claims Act creates incentives for providers to change the way they conduct health care."

Ventry looked directly at the impact paying large rewards in the IRS whistleblower program. He looked at the fallout from UBS whistleblower Bradley Birkenfeld's disclosures after Birkenfeld was paid a historic $104 million reward for revealing the ways in which UBS encouraged American citizens to dodge their taxes:

> "[T]hanks to one of 'the biggest whistleblowers of all time,' the U.S. government . . . received: $780 million and the names of 250 high-dollar Americans with secret accounts as part of a deferred prosecution agreement (DPA) with UBS; another 4,450 names and accounts of U.S. citizens provided as part of a joint settlement between the U.S. and Swiss governments; more than 120 criminal indictments of U.S. taxpayers and tax advisors . . . more than $5.5 billion collected from the IRS Offshore Voluntary Disclosure Program (OVDP), with untold tens of billions of dollars still payable due to only a quarter of the 39,000 OVDP cases being closed . . . All because one person blew the tax whistle."

As explained by Ventry, the deterrent effect of Birkenfeld's massive award achieved unprecedented reforms concerning illegal offshore banking, money laundering, and tax evasion.

Officials within the Swiss banking industry quickly realized the impact that paying a whistleblower a $104 million award would have on other employees working in that industry. Days after the Birkenfeld award was announced, bankers and their consultants held a major industry meeting in Geneva, Switzerland. At this meeting, the attendees "seethed" at Birkenfeld and attacked his "total lack of morality" for blowing the whistle on them.

According to a reporter from Agence France-Presse who attended the meeting, Birkenfeld had "driven the nail into the heart of the once seemingly invincible Swiss bank secrecy" system. A respected banking consultant reportedly declared that their U.S. client offshore banking program was "over."

The day after the Birkenfeld award was announced, the publication SwissInfo reported on the reaction to the award in the Swiss newspapers, and published the following summaries of multiple Swiss press stories:

> "Zurich's Tages-Anzeiger went further describing it as a "seductive offer for bankers." "This enormous reward show how the U.S. are raising the stakes in their tax fight with Switzerland . . . in promising such high compensation the IRS are hoping that more incriminating material is handed over.
>
> The French-speaking daily Le Temps agreed that Birkenfeld's huge reward could encourage other bank employees to follow his example."

From a cost-benefit analysis, the benefits of paying large rewards overwhelmingly outweigh any alleged costs associated with these payments. Awards are paid only if the whistleblower's information helps to detect criminal activity, activity that would remain unknown to law enforcement but for the whistleblower.

An effective whistleblower program creates a win-win-win-win scenario: the government wins by being able to police illegality; the whistleblower wins because he or she can obtain compensation; the public wins because a criminal is prosecuted and monies obtained from fines and sanctions are returned to the taxpayers; the markets win because potential bad actors are deterred from committing crimes, permitting fair competition and long-term savings to investors. Paying large rewards, with no caps, is the key to a truly successful whistleblower reward program.

The SEC's final rule on the cap issue will send a powerful message to the markets. Will it be one of deterrence, or will it signal or will it signal a retreat from a willingness to use one of the most effective regulatory tools to deter corruption in the markets?

> *"Under the whistleblower program,*
> *awards in a single enforcement*
> *action as high as $114 million have*
> *been paid."*

Law Firms Have a Fiscal Interest in Maintaining High Whistleblower Rewards

Mike Delikat and Renee Phillips

In this viewpoint by Mike Delikat and Renee Philips, the authors wonder if whistleblower rewards have gotten too high. In light of whistleblower payments exceeding $100 million, the U.S. Securities and Exchange Commission (SEC) has proposed laws that would curtail whistleblower payments in certain instances. Prominent whistleblower attorney Jordan A. Thomas has challenged those proposals, arguing that lowering payments arbitrarily may cause some whistleblowers not to come forward. Delikat and Phillips note that Thomas himself stands to make millions in legal fees through his representation of whistleblower clients. They conclude by stating that the SEC will vigorously defend its proposal to modify awards. Michael Delikat is a partner in the New York office of Orrick's Global Employment Law Practice and the founder of the firm's Whistleblower Task Force. Renee Phillips is a partner in Orrick's New York office and co-head of the firm's Whistleblower Task Force.

As you read, consider the following questions:

1. What does Rule 21-F6 state with respect to whistleblower awards?
2. On what grounds is Thomas challenging Rule 21-F6?
3. How do law firms stand to gain monetarily in whistleblower cases?

On January 13, 2021, prominent whistleblower attorney and a principal architect of the Dodd-Frank Act whistleblower program, Jordan A. Thomas, filed a complaint against the U.S. Securities and Exchange Commission ("SEC" or "Commission") seeking a declaratory judgment that certain provisions of the SEC's recent whistleblower program amendments are invalid and cannot be enforced. Specifically, the complaint challenges the SEC's "clarification" of its authority to limit the size and number of certain whistleblower awards.

Under Dodd-Frank, the Commission pays a monetary award to a whistleblower that provides information to the SEC that leads to an enforcement action in an amount equal to but not less than 10% and not more than 30% of the monetary sanctions imposed by the SEC. Under Rule 21-F6, the agency calculates whistleblower awards in that 10-30% range by assigning an award percentage based on an array of positive and negative factors. The SEC then issues an award by multiplying the award percentage by the total monetary sanctions that the SEC collected.

Under the whistleblower program, awards in a single enforcement action as high as $114 million have been paid. Thomas states that his clients have received some of the largest whistleblower awards in history, with three of his clients' cases involving monetary sanctions in excess of $100 million.

The SEC voiced concerns in 2018 that excessively large awards could deplete the Investor Protection Fund. As a result, the SEC originally proposed a revised Rule 21F-6 in 2018 that would have expressly provided the Commission with the ability to make downward adjustments in connection with large awards where the monetary sanctions equaled or exceeded $100 million as long as the award payout did not fall below $30 million. However, the SEC ultimately scrapped the proposed rule and instead clarified in the new rules that it has always had the authority and discretion to consider the total dollar payout when applying the award criteria and adjust downward for large awards as reasonably necessary.

In addition, under the prior Rule 21F-3, the SEC would pay awards based on amounts collected in "related actions" and defined "related action" as a "judicial or administrative action that is brought by [specified agencies or self-regulatory organizations], and . . . based on the same original information that the whistleblower voluntarily provided to the Commission." The SEC's recent amendments revised Rule 21F-3 to award information provided in a "related action" "only if the Commission finds . . . that its whistleblower program has the more direct or relevant connection to the action." Further, the Final Rule 21F-3 prevents whistleblowers from receiving an award if they have already been granted an award by another agency or if they have been denied an award by another agency's whistleblower program.

According to Mr. Thomas's complaint, the previous rules encouraged whistleblowers to come forward by guaranteeing that those individuals who acted properly would be awarded accordingly and would not have their awards unfairly and arbitrarily diminished. In his complaint, he argues that this "clarification" to Rule 21F-6 is unlawful under the Administrative Procedure Act ("APA") for at least five reasons: (1) the Final Rule was not a "logical outgrowth" of the proposed rule; (2) the SEC enacted the rule without acknowledging that it was changing its position; (3) the SEC failed to weigh the costs and benefits of the Final Rule; (4) the SEC adopted the rule without providing a reasoned explanation and despite the harms it will cause the whistleblower program; and (5) the SEC had no statutory authority to enact the rule. Furthermore, the complaint alleges the amendments to Rule 21F-3 are unlawful under the APA because (1) the SEC had no

THE SEC AWARD TWO WHISTLEBLOWERS $40 MILLION

The Securities and Exchange Commission today announced awards of approximately $40 million to two whistleblowers whose information and assistance contributed to the success of an SEC enforcement action.

The first whistleblower, whose information caused the opening of the investigation and exposed difficult-to-detect violations, will receive an award of approximately $32 million. The first whistleblower also provided substantial assistance to the staff, including identifying witnesses and helping the staff to understand complex fact patterns. The second whistleblower, who submitted important new information during the course of the investigation but waited several years to report to the Commission, will receive an award of approximately $8 million.

"Today's whistleblowers underscore the importance of the SEC's whistleblower program to the agency's enforcement efforts," said Emily Pasquinelli, Acting Chief of the SEC's Office of the Whistleblower. "These whistleblowers reported critical information that aided the Commission's investigation and provided extensive, ongoing cooperation that helped the Commission to stop the wrongdoing and protect the capital markets."

The SEC has awarded approximately $1.1 billion to 218 individuals since issuing its first award in 2012. All payments are made out of an investor protection fund established by Congress that is financed entirely through monetary sanctions paid to the SEC by securities law violators. No money has been taken or withheld from harmed investors to pay whistleblower awards. Whistleblowers may be eligible for an award when they voluntarily provide the SEC with original, timely, and credible information that leads to a successful enforcement action. Whistleblower awards can range from 10-30% of the money collected when the monetary sanctions exceed $1 million.

As set forth in the Dodd-Frank Act, the SEC protects the confidentiality of whistleblowers and does not disclose information that could reveal a whistleblower's identity.

"SEC Awards $40 Million to Two Whistleblowers," U.S. Securities and Exchange Commission, October 15, 2021.

statutory authority to enact the changes and (2) the SEC adopted the rule without providing a reasoned explanation and despite the harms it will cause the whistleblower program.

As the complaint asserts, "[T]he potential for large monetary awards is the primary motivation for individuals to blow the whistle to law enforcement and regulatory authorities" and the challenged rule amendments "turn the Commission into a kind of casino that aggressively courts high-rollers with the promise of large jackpots but reserves the right to lower their winnings if those winnings get 'too large.'" Further, the complaint surmises that would-be whistleblowers may weigh the costs and benefits of the revised whistleblower program and choose not to report possible securities violations to the SEC if they are worried their awards may be adjusted downwards or denied outright under the related action rules, ultimately reducing the number of individuals who report.

Certainly for the whistleblower bar, significant contingent legal fees are at stake. The complaint notes that Thomas currently has nine whistleblower clients awaiting a final determination of entitlement to an award from the SEC, and that given the monetary sanctions collected, his clients collectively are eligible for awards of more than $300 million. On each of these potential awards, Thomas' firm will receive a contingency fee, and Plaintiff Thomas will receive incentive compensation for recovering the award on behalf of his client.

This is the first action attacking the Final Rule and no doubt will be met with a vigorous defense by the SEC. We will monitor the progress of this action and questions of standing (i.e., whether lawyers that represent whistleblowers have standing to challenge this Final Rule) and whether the Final Rule passes muster under the APA.

> *"Our legal history is replete with examples of sweeping reform generated, not only by legislative bodies, but also by individuals and their lawyers making themselves heard through the legal system."*

Whistleblowers Can Help Enact Reform

Reuben A. Guttman

In this viewpoint, Rueben Guttman discusses the concept that individuals can bring about great change in society through monitoring and reporting inequities. Individual efforts to bring about change are important when government officials will not act due to a lack of resources or political pressure. Whistleblowers ask hard questions and expose impropriety. But such efforts are not always rewarded; whistleblowers are not valued by society as they should be, according to Guttman. Guttman discusses the complexities involved when a whistleblower reported former President Trump's alleged efforts to coerce the Ukrainian government into providing damaging information on his political opponent, President Biden. This scenario is an important example, Guttman suggests, of how even a president can be held accountable by an individual citizen. Reuben Guttman is a founding member of Guttman, Buschner & Brooks, PLLC where his practice involves complex litigation and class actions.

"Whistleblowers and the Rule of Law," by Reuben A. Guttman, American Constitution Society, October 21, 2019. Reprinted by permission.

As you read, consider the following questions:

1. In what important legal cases has an individual brought about reform?
2. What was the first whistleblower law enacted in the U.S.?
3. How does Guttman use the analogy of a booster rocket to describe whistleblowers?

In the United States, law students learn that law is both substance and process. Substance is the proscription or obligation and process is the mechanism for enforcing compliance. Absent a compliance enforcement mechanism, the substance is of no consequence. An unenforced law is tantamount to no law at all.

Americans obsess about the process mechanism's fairness and enforcement logistics. Consistent with our entrenched mistrust for government, evidenced by the checks and balances of our three-branch government, we do not leave matters solely in the hands of politicians. Our laws also allow for citizen participation in enforcement. Major pieces of legislation including our civil rights, environmental, antitrust, and housing laws allow individuals to bring suits to enforce law. Not only do citizen suits leverage compliance enforcement, they also ensure compliance when government prosecutors lack the resources or the political motivation to enforce the law.

Our legal history is replete with examples of sweeping reform generated, not only by legislative bodies, but also by individuals and their lawyers making themselves heard through the legal system. Landmark cases including *Brown v. Board of Education of Topeka*[1], *Loving v. Virginia*[2], and *Cleveland Board of Education v. LaFleur*[3] were initiated by individuals and led to the eradication of discriminatory practices. These cases are testaments to the power of one person represented by (at times) overworked and inexperienced lawyers motivated by the fear of failure and the passion to do good.

Our rule of law is special because it provides mechanisms for individuals to effectuate change. Such mechanisms are essential when elected officials fail to act or when the accepted practices of reputable institutions—including large corporations—harm the voiceless. The people who ask hard questions and shed light on impropriety are called "whistleblowers." A myriad of laws protect whistleblowers from retaliation and some laws—including the qui tam provisions of the federal False Claims Act—reward considerable risk-taking. We owe a debt of gratitude to those who stuck their neck out and blew the whistle; they are responsible for safer products, a healthier environment, and a more trustworthy government.

Now Congress—relying on a confidential report made by a whistleblower to the Office of the Inspector General of the Intelligence Community—is investigating whether President Trumpsought the help of the Ukrainian government to investigate his political opponent, Joe Biden. The process established by the rule of law is now in motion. The inspector general investigated the whistleblower's concerns and the matter has moved forward to another branch of government for oversight and possible corrective action. This is fully consistent federal law.[4]

For the important role they play, whistleblowers should be considered more American than apple pie. But that is not how they are always treated. Consider President Trump's tweet from October 9, 2019: "[t]he Whistleblower's facts have been so incorrect about my no pressure conversation with the Ukrainian President, and now the conflict of interest and involvement with a Democrat Candidate, that he or she should be exposed and questioned properly. This is no Whistleblower..."

President Trump fails to appreciate the process governing whistleblowing, let alone intelligence community whistleblowing. If he wanted to educate himself, he need look no farther than his own appointee's website. The Office of the Director of National Intelligence website contains this message from Inspector General Michael Atkinson:

"Whistleblowing has a long history in this country. Over 240 years ago, on July 30, 1778, the Continental Congress unanimously enacted the first whistleblower legislation in the United States, proclaiming that 'it is the duty of all persons in service of the United States, as well as all other the inhabitants thereof, to give the earliest information to Congress or other proper authority of any misconduct, frauds or misdemeanors committed by any officers or persons in the service of these states, which comes to their knowledge.' To this day, Federal law (including the Constitution, rules, and regulations) encourages, consistent with the protection of classified information (including sources and methods of detection of classified information), the honest and good faith reporting of misconduct, fraud, misdemeanors, and other crimes to the appropriate authority at the earliest time possible."

Consistent with efforts to chill the whistleblowing tradition, the president of United States now demands disclosure of the whistleblower's identity, an examination under oath, and exposure of biases. Here again, the president fails to appreciate the role of whistleblowers. Sometimes—as is the case here—whistleblowers are merely a catalyst causing regulators or legislators to scrutinize a situation, gather evidence, and judge the facts against the law. The whistleblower may raise an issue based on information that would be inadmissible under the Federal Rules of Evidence. It is the ensuing investigation, document collection, and witness interviews that matter. Afterwards, whistleblower testimony or bias is irrelevant.

By analogy, the whistleblower is no more than a booster rocket propelling the space shuttle into orbit, or in the legal world, a trial. A whistleblower may very well be motivated by bias; perhaps they did not get all the facts right. Yet, what is put before the trier of fact is not necessarily whistleblower testimony, but evidence gathered because a whistleblower caused an investigation.

In the current situation, the whistleblower's allegations generated enough concern to motivate an investigation of what may be unimpeachable admissible evidence. Whatever the outcome of the Congressional investigation, we will have seen the rule of law at work, with its role for individuals and countervailing branches of government. It is a system where—on any given day—the nation's most powerful person can be called to account by an individual who thoughtfully raised questions. For those studying these current events, this is once again a lesson in how individual whistleblowers are essential to our legal tradition.

Notes

[1] Brown v. Bd. of Ed. of Topeka, Shawnee Cty., Kan., 347 U.S. 483, 74 S. Ct. 686, 98 L. Ed. 873 (1954), supplemented sub nom. Brown v. Bd. of Educ. of Topeka, Kan., 349 U.S. 294, 75 S. Ct. 753, 99 L. Ed. 1083 (1955).

[2] Loving v. Virginia, 388 U.S. 1, 87 S. Ct. 1817, 18 L. Ed. 2d 1010 (1967).

[3] Cleveland Bd. of Educ. v. LaFleur, 414 U.S. 632, 94 S. Ct. 791, 39 L. Ed. 2d 52 (1974).

[4] 50 U.S.C. § 3033.

Periodical and Internet Sources Bibliography

The following articles have been selected to supplement the diverse views presented in this chapter.

"Whistleblowing—A Rewarding Act?" Protect-Advice, April 21, 2022. https://protect-advice.org.uk/whistleblowing-a-rewarding-act/.

Elletta Sangrey Callahan and Terry Morehead Dworkin, "Do Good and Get Rich: Financial Incentives for Whistleblowing and the False Claims Act and the False Claims Act," *Villanova Law Review*, 1992. https://digitalcommons.law.villanova.edu/cgi/viewcontent.cgi?referer=&httpsredir=1&article=2777&context=vlr.

Stephen Conmy, "Should Whistleblowers Be Rewarded?" The Corporate Governance Institute, October 24, 2021. https://www.thecorporategovernanceinstitute.com/insights/news-analysis/should-whistleblowers-be-rewarded/.

EQS Integrity Team, "A Closer Look at The Ethics Behind Whistleblower Rewards," Integrity Line, September 13, 2022. https://www.integrityline.com/expertise/blog/ethics-behind-whistleblower-rewards/.

Giovanni Immordino, Giancarlo Spagnolo, and Paolo Buccirossi, "Whistleblower rewards, false reports, and corporate fraud," VoxEU, October 11, 2017. https://cepr.org/voxeu/columns/whistleblower-rewards-false-reports-and-corporate-fraud.

Stephen M. Kohn. "Should Whistleblower Reward Laws be Capped?" Promarket, August 30, 2020. https://www.promarket.org/2020/08/30/should-whistleblower-reward-laws-be-capped/.

Kohn, Kohn, and Calapinto, LLP, '$200 Million Whistleblower Reward Sparks Nationwide Debate,' November 23, 2021, JD Supra. https://www.jdsupra.com/legalnews/200-million-whistleblower-reward-sparks-8152254/.

Brandon J. Mark, "What Really Motivates Whistleblowers? Misperceptions Abound…," Parsons, Behle, and Latimer, January 13, 2015. https://parsonsbehle.com/insights/what-really-motivates-whistleblowers-misperceptions-abound.

Mengqi Sun, "SEC Whistleblower Awards Program Might Have a Revolving-Door Problem, Study Says," the *Wall Street Journal*.

August 25, 2022. https://www.wsj.com/articles/sec-whistleblower-awards-program-might-have-a-revolving-door-problem-study-says-11661419801?mod=hp_minor_pos10.

Robert Towey, "Whistleblowers Ultimately Help Their Companies Perform Better, a New Study Shows," CNBC, November 24, 2018. https://www.cnbc.com/2018/11/24/whistleblowers-ultimately-help-their-companies-perform-better-study.html.

Kyle Welch and Stephen Stubben "Throw Out Your Assumptions About Whistleblowing," *Harvard Business Review*, January 14, 2020. https://hbr.org/2020/01/throw-out-your-assumptions-about-whistleblowing.

The Whistleblower Law Firm, "Whistleblower Rewards: A Reason for Taking a Risk," HG.org. https://www.hg.org/legal-articles/whistleblower-rewards-a-reason-for-taking-a-risk-30348.

Jason Zuckerman and Matt Stock, "One Billion Reasons Why the SEC Whistleblower-Reward Program Is Effective," *Forbes,* July 18, 2017. https://www.forbes.com/sites/realspin/2017/07/18/one-billion-reasons-why-the-sec-whistleblower-reward-program-is-effective/?sh=3d1e6d1b3009.

OPPOSING
VIEWPOINTS®
SERIES

CHAPTER 2

Should Whistleblowers Be Protected?

Chapter Preface

Whistleblowing is a risky proposition. Though there are whistleblower protection laws in place, their effectiveness varies greatly depending on the type of whistleblowing activity. Many "relators," as whistleblowers are often called, fall through the cracks. Retaliation by one's organization is a major concern for potential whistleblowers. According to Harvard Business School Professor Jonas Heenes, "…it's very difficult to prevent retaliation just with provisions that say you are not allowed to retaliate."[1]

Most whistleblowers do not inform on their corporation or government as a first recourse. Instead, they often report malfeasance to others in their organization: co-workers, bosses, executives, etc. Actual whistleblowing often occurs when their concerns are met with apathy, opposition, or even retaliation. Relators may then feel that they have no choice but to voice their concerns to the media or consult with an attorney to open a whistleblower case.

Most attorneys will counsel a client not to go to their organization first, but in many cases, it is too late. Attorneys also stress the importance of whistleblower anonymity. The National Whistleblower Center (NWC) advises potential relators that "the best way for a whistleblower to prevent retaliation is to remain anonymous."[2] If a company does not know who the whistleblower is, it will be harder for them to retaliate.

Retaliation measures, large or small, are commonplace. The NWC notes that "According to a study from the Bradley University Center for Cybersecurity, nearly two-thirds of the whistleblowers surveyed experienced some form of retaliation, including termination, forced retirement, negative performance evaluation, social ostracism, and blacklisting from other jobs in their field."[3]

If relators are not careful, they may ruin their careers.

One of the more high-profile recent whistleblower cases involved Theranos, a company founded by tech golden girl Elizabeth Holmes. The company claimed that it had created blood tests requiring only a finger prick. With just a few drops of blood, the company could run hundreds of tests to determine patient illnesses. Based on this prospectus, the company was able to raise $700 million from investors, including billionaires such as NewsCorp's Rupert Murdoch and Oracle's Larry Ellison.

Erika Cheung, a Theranos lab assistant fresh out of college, began to suspect something was wrong at Theranos, and that its technology could not do what Holmes said it could. Theranos was defrauding its patients and investors. Cheung attempted to report her findings internally, but was met with stonewalling and derision. She realized that Holmes knew the limitations of their blood tests. "It was clear that there was an open secret within Theranos that this technology simply didn't exist," said Tyler Shultz, a former Theranos employee who shared Cheung's concerns.[4]

But Theranos executives had stifled dissent through intimidation and fear. "There are only a few cases that I know of where some actually did raise concerns to the level of Elizabeth [Holmes] or [COO] Sunny [Balwani], and they were pretty much fired right on the spot," said Shultz. "No one was motivated to speak up. Their culture of fear worked for them for a long time."[5] Holmes had good reason for keeping the fraud going: at the peak of Theranos' "success," the college drop-out was worth over $4 billion.

Cheung eventually resigned from Theranos and took her concerns to the *Wall Street Journal's* John Carreyrou, who broke the story. It was the beginning of the end for Theranos.

For her attempt to bring the truth to light, Cheung received threats from Theranos. Even after she had resigned from the company, she was allegedly being surveilled by Theranos. On one occasion a letter was hand-delivered to her that threatened legal action if she didn't immediately cease "making false and defamatory statements about the Company." The letter was delivered to an address where no one but her close friend knew she was staying.

According to Carreyrou, she stayed in the house the entire weekend that followed, "too terrified to set foot outside."[6]

It is clear from Cheung's story and countless others that whether informing on a corporation, a government, a police department, or any other organization, relators must go in with a plan. Protecting oneself is a must, and until there are better laws protecting whistleblowers, they are placing themselves in harm's way. When Cheung was asked, "Would you do it again?" She replied that she would have, but that she would have done some things differently. "Would I have done it better? Yeah, I definitely would have hired a lawyer." [7]

Notes

1. April White, "Truth Be Told: Unpacking the Risks of Whistleblowing," Harvard Business School Working Knowledge, December 10, 2021. https://hbswk.hbs.edu/item/truth-be-told-unpacking-the-risks-of-whistleblowing.

2. "Whistleblower Confidentiality," National Whistleblower Center. https://www.whistleblowers.org/whistleblower-confidentiality/.

3. *Ibid.*

4. Bobby Allyn, "Theranos Whistleblower Celebrated Elizabeth Holmes Verdict by 'Popping Champagne'," NPR, January 5, 2022. https://www.npr.org/2022/01/05/1070474663/theranos-whistleblower-tyler-shultz-elizabeth-holmes-verdict-champagne.

5. Stephen Kurczy, "Lessons from the Theranos Whistleblower," Columbia Business School, April 8, 2019. https://www8.gsb.columbia.edu/articles/ideas-work/lessons-theranos-whistleblower.

6. John Carreyrou, *Bad Blood: Secrets and Lies in a Silicon Valley Startup.* New York, NY: Alfred A. Knopf, 2018.

7. Rob Pegoraro, "Theranos Whistleblower on Lessons Learned: 'I Would Have Hired a Lawyer'," *PCMag,* September 15, 2022. https://www.pcmag.com/news/theranos-whistleblower-on-lessons-learned-i-would-have-hired-a-lawyer.

> "Referring to legitimate whistleblowing as leaking gives cover to actions that support the rhetorical implication that such speech is something unlawful rather than protected."

Calling Whistleblowers "Leakers" Erodes Their Rights

Dana Gold

Dana Gold writes that when the government classifies whistleblowers as leakers, this classification has the effect of putting whistleblowers in harm's way. When it comes to government whistleblowers, Gold states, whistleblower protections for intelligence community employees are notoriously weak, and they are even weaker for intelligence contractors. Whistleblowers who act in good faith are thus placed in extreme jeopardy, even when their disclosures are deemed essential to protecting the public's interest in accountable government. Aggressive prosecutions of government whistleblowers feed the narrative that the whistleblower has committed a crime, even if their revelations are not considered classified information. Gold asserts that in a political climate where corruption and criminal behavior are considered the norm, whistleblowers are needed more than ever, and they must be protected. Dana Gold is the Director of Education for the Government Accountability Project at the American Constitution Society.

"Leaking v. Whistleblowing: Using Rhetoric to Erode Rights," by Dana Gold, Senior Counsel, Government Accountability Project. Reprinted by permission.

As you read, consider the following questions:

1. What is the difference between calling someone a
   "whistleblower" and a "leaker"?
2. How do the Whistleblower Protection Act (WPA) and the
   Whistleblower Protection Enhancement Act (WPEA)
   laws protect whistleblowers?
3. How does using the inflammatory rhetorical term, "leaker"
   endanger whistleblowers, according to Gold?

On March 28, 2018, FBI agent Terry Albury was charged under the Espionage Act with leaking classified FBI policy manuals to *The Intercept* that describe the FBI's use of race and religion to decide who to investigate and surveillance tactics used to obtain journalists' phone records without a judge-issued warrant or subpoena. Albury is the Trump Administration's most recent target in their mission to prosecute so-called leakers. Reality Winner, an NSA contractor and the first person charged by the Trump administration with leaking classified information to the press (again *The Intercept)*, is in jail awaiting trial for sharing a classified report about Russian cyberattacks executed to interfere with the 2016 presidential election.

But we should not call Winner and Albury leakers. They are whistleblowers.[1]

The term leaker, when used by those in political power, is often used to imply any person releasing unauthorized information is doing something wrong and possibly criminal. Referring to legitimate whistleblowing as leaking gives cover to actions that support the rhetorical implication that such speech is something unlawful rather than protected.

In Albury and Winner's cases, as members of the intelligence community, things are more complicated.

Whistleblower protection laws, though an imperfect patchwork of protections, seek to *encourage* disclosures of evidence of wrongdoing by offering protections from retaliation (and in some cases, to those who would disclose financial fraud, a potential financial reward for reporting violations). The whistleblower patchwork is overwhelmingly an employment law scheme, reflecting the fact that employees are in the best position to witness problems, promote compliance, and facilitate enforcement.

The Whistleblower Protection Act (WPA) of 1989 (amended by the Whistleblower Protection Enhancement Act (WPEA) of 2012) is the primary law that gives non-intelligence federal workers the right to report serious wrongdoing. The WPA extends protection from retaliation to employees for disclosing information both internally, such as to co-workers, managers, an agency Inspector General, etc., as well as externally, such as to Congress, regulators, watchdog organizations, and the press. That both internal and external disclosures are protected recognizes that to promote the normative and instrumental value of encouraging employee disclosures, laws should address the two (unfortunately legitimate) reasons employees stay silent in the face of wrongdoing: fear of reprisal and fear of futility, or that nothing will come from speaking out. Though most employees raise concerns internally first—over 95%—they will go outside of the organization if they feel the issue must be addressed and that internal disclosures will be ineffective and/or be met with reprisal.

The WPA and WPEA (which were, like all federal whistleblower laws, passed with bipartisan, unanimous congressional support) articulate a useful standard to evaluate the content that would rise to the level of a protected whistleblowing disclosure: information an employee reasonably believes evidences a violation of law, rule or regulation; gross mismanagement; gross waste of funds; abuse of authority; a substantial and specific danger to public health or safety; or scientific censorship that would result in these forms of misconduct.

All of the disclosures by the "leakers" prosecuted above would likely meet the standard of wrongdoing categorized in the WPA deemed essential to protecting the public's interest in accountable government—FBI investigation practices that could violate civil rights and liberties; foreign interference with U.S. elections; unconstitutional electronic surveillance of American citizens; and illegal torture. In other words, the leaking also constituted whistleblowing.

Whistleblower protections for intelligence community employees are notoriously weak, and even weaker for intelligence contractors. Avenues for disclosure too are limited, often only to the agency responsible for the alleged wrongdoing, with evidence that sometimes with those charged with investigating concerns instead investigating and retaliating against the whistleblower. Penalties are severe and there is no public interest defense available to whistleblowers charged with releasing classified information (in contrast to many other democratic countries).

But the absence of meaningful legal protections or safe, effective avenues for disclosure reveals a hole in the legal patchwork of whistleblower protections, not that the disclosure itself is not the kind that is essential to ensuring that democratic institutions—Congress, the courts, executive branch agencies, the press, civil society, and a concerned electorate—promote accountability.

This is why Albury, Winner, Edward Snowden, Thomas Drake and John Kiriakou should be considered whistleblowers.

The aggressive prosecutions of intelligence whistleblowers using the rhetoric of "leakers" feeds into the narrative that whistleblowing is a crime, or a threat to national security, even though most leaks of information, and most whistleblowing, have nothing to do with national security or intelligence matters and do not involve classified information.

Whistleblowers by the very nature of raising a concern are making "unauthorized" disclosures, but this is a legally protected right. Further, in a dysfunctional political environment hostile to truth and truth-tellers, many federal employees will raise concerns externally, often attempting to keep their identity anonymous to try to avoid reprisal while seeking effective reform through the media or an advocacy group. But to call this activity "leaking" rather than "whistleblowing" may give pause to the career civil servant who has witnessed serious misconduct but may feel both confused and chilled by the frightening rhetoric. By conflating "leaking" with "whistleblowing," those who stand the most to lose by having their abuses disclosed are deliberately undermining both the normative value of whistleblower protection laws and policies as well as their practical effectiveness by chilling rather than encouraging disclosure.

The rhetorical move legitimizes illegitimate tactics being used to silence employees, such as anti-leak training being ordered for all federal employees, not just those in the intelligence agencies; directives ordering employees to seek pre-approval by legal affairs or public information offices before speaking with any outside parties; nondisclosure agreements signed by White House staff barring lifetime release of "confidential" information; posters hung in the Department of Energy reminding employees that "Every Leak Makes Us Weak;" environmental agencies barring employees from speaking at conferences referencing climate change; heightened review of FOIA requests submitted by journalists or public interest watchdogs, possibly to ferret out potential internal sources (the tactic used by the FBI to identify agent Albury through *The Intercept's* FOIA request); and Secretary of Education Betsy DeVos seeking guidance on her suggestion to prosecute employees who release unclassified budget documents to the press.

Most of these moves are illegal and unenforceable on a range of grounds. But in the aggregate, they create a powerful chilling effect on speech of public interest concern—protected whistleblowing—under the guise of combatting "leaks."

Admittedly, the leaking v. whistleblowing distinction is indeed complicated in the national security context, and there has been substantial and excellent analysis on the issue by many terrific legal scholars, including Heidi Kitrosser, Mary-Rose Papandrea, David Pozen and others. However, weaknesses in legal protections and effective avenues for disclosure of classified matters of serious public concern (not to mention the well-documented problem of over classification that exacerbates the issue) have created the conditions that allow those in political power to exploit the few but graphic examples of national security whistleblowing as "illegal leaking" to chill whistleblowing in other contexts.

In a political climate where corruption and secrecy rather than honesty and transparency are the norm, whistleblowers are needed more than ever. Efforts to undermine our flawed but nonetheless essential laws that encourage whistleblowing must be exposed and confronted for the deliberately disparaging and dishonest rhetoric, indeed propaganda, that they are.

Notes

[1] Other famous intelligence whistleblowers similarly labeled as "leakers" include Edward Snowden, whose disclosures to *The Guardian* of the NSA's mass surveillance of U.S. citizens' electronic communications made him the most high profile "leaker" since Daniel Ellsberg's "leak" of the Pentagon Papers to the *New York Times*; Thomas Drake, whose internal and external disclosures about unconstitutional mass surveillance (none of which, despite aggressive prosecution efforts, included unclassified disclosures to the press) preceded Edward Snowden's and informed his decision to "leak" in the manner he did; and John Kiriakou, who, after revealing on *ABC News* that the CIA had an official torture program that included waterboarding, was jailed for revealing the name of a covert agent to a reporter (no one who actually conducted torture, issued the policy, or destroyed evidence of the illegal practice was prosecuted).

> *"You must take all possible actions to preserve your anonymity. You need to be aware of the social and technical risks, and take the right countermeasures to protect yourself."*

Leakers Need to Protect Themselves

WildLeaks

In this viewpoint directed at prospective whistleblowers, the authors counsel those who are contemplating coming forward with improper corporate behavior to guard their anonymity above all else. They offer tips to whistleblowers as to how to come forward carefully and discretely. If whistleblowers follow the tips offered by WildLeaks, they should be protected, but the authors caution that they can never be 100 percent certain of being safe. Whistleblowing, they suggest, is a dangerous business and must be entered into with extreme caution. WildLeaks is the world's first whistleblowing initiative dedicated to environmental crime. The mission of WildLeaks is to receive and evaluate anonymous information regarding environmental crime and transform that information into concrete actions.

As you read, consider the following questions:

1. What are some specific tips that the authors offer to potential whistleblowers?

"Possible Risks & How to Protect Yourself", WildLeaks. Reprinted by permission. WildLeaks and Earth League International (ELI).

2. Why are computers never completely safe as a medium for reporting, according to the viewpoint?

3. Why must potential whistleblowers be computer proficient?

When submitting sensitive information, you must consider the risks involved in taking that action to reveal the truth, as you may be subject to retaliation by parties that do not like what you have to say.

That is why you must take all possible actions to preserve your anonymity. You need to be aware of the social and technical risks, and take the right countermeasures to protect yourself. The most applicable protection strategies depend on the scenario, especially those related to social risks.

First of all, when you leak or share sensitive information, there are always some risks involved that could threaten your anonymity. When considering the information that you want to share, determine whether sending us that information in a Confidential fully encrypted way (via HTTPS) is enough. If it is not and you need stronger anonymity, we suggest you download and install the Tor Browser so that you are able to anonymously access the Internet and WildLeaks. Naturally, DO NOT submit sensitive information from your work site or with computers belonging to your employer. Do it from home and with a private computer, or from an Internet cafe.

It's easy and quick to install the Tor Browser.

The following risks overview and series of hints and tips will help you protect yourself:

Social/General Risks

The most important thing to consider is what can happen after your leak/submit information and it is used for an investigation or by the media. Please think about the following before submitting any information:

- Are you the only person who has access to the information that you have submitted?
- If the submitted information reaches public attention, will someone ask you something about it? Is the information directly traceable to you only?
- Are you aware that after the information is used for an investigation or published by the media, people around you may ask about the leaked information?
- Can you handle the psychological pressure of an internal or external investigation (someone asking you about the information) about the submission?

To better protect yourself you should, at the very least, take the following set of actions:

- Before you make a submission to WildLeaks, do not disclose your intention to anyone.
- After you make a submission, do not tell anyone about what you have done.
- If the news about the submission gets out to public media, be really careful when expressing your opinion or disclosing further information about it with anyone.
- Be sure that there's no surveillance systems (cameras or other) in the place where you acquire and submit the information.
- Do not look around on search engines or news media websites for the information you submitted (this would reveal that you knew about it earlier).
- These are just a set of social protection actions that you must consider as a whistleblower.

Technical Risks

You must be aware of the fact that while using a computer and the Internet to exchange information, most of the actions you take leave traces (computer logs) that could lead an investigator to identify where you are and who you are.

For this reason you must consider risk mitigation strategies and adopt very specific precautions to avoid leaving technological traces about your actions.

You may leave computer's traces while:

- Researching the information to be submitted
- Acquiring the information to be submitted
- Reading this web page
- Submitting the information to us
- Exchanging data with receivers of your submission
- Downloading software, including the Tor Browser

Technological protection actions could be the most tricky to understand due to the underlying technical complexity of today's computing and networking systems. To achieve a 100% guarantee of security from a technical perspective, you need to be computer-proficient enough to fully understand all the risks.

However, by strictly following the procedures and tips reported below, you should be safe enough.

How can you protect yourself and improve your anonymity?

- Use the Tor Browser for "Anonymous Web Browsing." Click here to download it
- Use BleachBit that removes many traces of your computer.
- Upload information from your personal computer, not the one at your employer/company
- Keep the receipt code that you receive from WildLeaks after uploading a submission in a safe place.
- Remove any information from your computer after the upload.
- If possible keep a copy of the uploaded information in a safe place not at work.
- After you upload the information make sure you leave no trace on the ICT systems and other devices, which can be used to understand your identity. For example, if you use a USB card/key, delete all the files that you uploaded and substitute them with other files like photos, videos and music.

- Please be aware of the metadata information that may be associated to the information that you have uploaded, such as author's name, date of writing, etc. You can use programs to remove the metadata from your files.

By applying the above-described procedures you should be safe enough. But safe enough doesn't mean 100% safe.

*"You have the right to file a
whistleblower complaint with
OSHA if you believe your employer
retaliated against you for exercising
your rights as an employee under
the whistleblower protection laws
enforced by OSHA."*

OSHA's Whistleblower Protection Program Helps Protect Those in Need

Occupational Safety and Health Administration

This viewpoint discusses the Occupational Safety and Health Administration's (OSHA) Whistleblower Protection Program and how it offers aid to those who have faced retaliation due to whistleblowing. Retaliation occurs when an employer takes any type of punitive action against someone who has informed on inappropriate practices. The viewpoint describes how to file a whistleblower complaint and what a whistleblower can expect during the process. At the conclusion of the resulting OSHA investigation, either a settlement can be reached, or the Department of Labor will file a complaint in district court to remedy the retaliation. OSHA's Whistleblower Protection Program enforces protections for employees who suffer retaliation for engaging in protected activities under more than 20 federal laws. OSHA's investigators are neutral fact finders; they do not work for either the complainant or respondent (employer). OSHA is a regulatory agency of the U.S. Department of Labor.

"The Whistleblower Protection Program," Whistleblowers.gov.

As you read, consider the following questions:

1. What are some of the acts of retaliation covered under whistleblower protections?
2. What types of evidence are useful for whistleblowers to keep?
3. How long do whistleblower investigations usually take?

OSHA's Whistleblower Protection Program enforces the whistleblower provisions of more than 20 whistleblower statutes protecting employees from retaliation for reporting violations of various workplace safety and health, airline, commercial motor carrier, consumer product, environmental, financial reform, food safety, health insurance reform, motor vehicle safety, nuclear, pipeline, public transportation agency, railroad, maritime, securities, tax, antitrust, and anti-money laundering laws and for engaging in other related protected activities.

Learn more about workplace retaliation and what it means, how to file a whistleblower complaint, how to create an anti-retaliation program, what to expect during a whistleblower investigation, and more below.

Retaliation

The whistleblower laws that OSHA enforces prohibit employers from retaliating against employees for engaging in activities protected under those laws.

What Is Retaliation?

Retaliation occurs when an employer (through a manager, supervisor, or administrator) fires an employee or takes any other type of adverse action against an employee for engaging in protected activity.

What Is an Adverse Action?

An adverse action is an action which would dissuade a reasonable employee from raising a concern about a possible violation or engaging in other related protected activity. Retaliation harms individual employees and can have a negative impact on overall employee morale. Because an adverse action can be subtle, such as excluding employees from important meetings, it may not always be easy to recognize.

Adverse actions may include actions such as:

- Firing or laying off
- Demoting
- Denying overtime or promotion
- Disciplining
- Denying benefits
- Failing to hire or rehire
- Intimidation or harassment
- Making threats
- Reassignment to a less desirable position or actions affecting prospects for promotion (such as excluding an employee from training meetings)
- Reducing or changing pay or hours
- More subtle actions, such as isolating, ostracizing, mocking, or falsely accusing the employee of poor performance
- Blacklisting (intentionally interfering with an employee's ability to obtain future employment)
- Constructive discharge (quitting when an employer makes working conditions intolerable due to the employee's protected activity)
- Reporting or threatening to report an employee to the police or immigration authorities

Are Temporary Workers Protected from Retaliation?

When a staffing agency supplies temporary workers to a business, both the staffing agency and its client (commonly referred to as the host employer) may be held legally responsible for retaliating against workers.

What Is an Example of Retaliation?

Example situation: A worker informed her employer that she called OSHA because she believed there was a fire hazard that her employer refused to fix. The worker had reported the fire hazard previously to her employer. A workplace practice existed which allowed all employees to swap shifts if they needed to take time off. The worker tried to swap shifts a few days after she told her employer that she called OSHA, but her employer did not allow her to swap. However, the other employees were still allowed to swap shifts.

Example analysis: Workers have a right to call OSHA to report an unsafe condition. Section 11(c) of the Occupational Safety and Health Act protects workers who file complaints with OSHA. By calling OSHA to complain about the fire hazard, the worker engaged in protected activity under one of the whistleblower laws administered by OSHA. She informed her employer that she called OSHA. Her employer denied her shift swap only a few days after being notified that she called OSHA. In addition, she was the only employee denied the ability to swap shifts. The denial of the shift swap is an adverse action. And, in this case, it appears that her employer denied her shift swap because she engaged in the protected activity. If the employer denied her request to swap because she called OSHA, then retaliation has occurred and the employer's actions violated section 11(c) of the Occupational Safety and Health Act.

Whistleblower Protections from the U.S. Government

The U.S. Department of Labor is an organization of diverse functions that carries out its mission through a number of offices and agencies. Five agencies enforce whistleblower and anti-retaliation laws.

Occupational Safety and Health Administration (OSHA)

With the Occupational Safety and Health Act of 1970, Congress created the Occupational Safety and Health Administration (OSHA) to ensure safe and healthful working conditions for workers by setting and enforcing standards and by providing training, outreach, education and assistance.

Mine Safety and Health Administration (MSHA)

The U.S. Department of Labor's Mine Safety and Health Administration (MSHA) helps to reduce deaths, injuries, and illnesses in the nation's mines with a variety of activities and programs. The agency develops and enforces safety and health rules for all U.S. mines, and provides technical, educational and other types of assistance to mine operators.

Office of Federal Contract Compliance Programs (OFCCP)

The Office of Federal Contract Compliance Programs (OFCCP), protects workers, promotes diversity and enforces the law. OFCCP holds those who do business with the federal government (contractors and subcontractors) responsible for complying with the legal requirement to take affirmative action and not discriminate on the basis of race, color, sex, sexual orientation, gender identity, religion, national origin, disability, or status as a protected veteran. In addition, contractors and subcontractors are prohibited from discharging or otherwise discriminating against applicants or employees who inquire about, discuss or disclose their compensation or that of others, subject to certain limitations.

Wage and Hour Division (WHD)

The Wage and Hour Division (WHD) mission is to promote and achieve compliance with labor standards to protect and enhance the welfare of the nation's workforce. The agency enforces federal minimum wage, overtime pay, recordkeeping, and child labor requirements of the Fair Labor Standards Act. WHD also enforces the Migrant and Seasonal Agricultural Worker Protection Act, the Employee Polygraph Protection Act, the Family and Medical Leave Act, wage garnishment provisions of the Consumer Credit Protection Act, and a number of employment standards and worker protections as provided in several immigration related statutes.

Veterans' Employment and Training Service (VETS)

The Veterans' Employment and Training Service prepares America's veterans, service members and their spouses, for meaningful careers, provide them with employment resources and expertise, protect their employment rights and promote their employment opportunities.

"Whistleblower protections," U.S. Department of Labor.

How to File a Whistleblower Complaint

You have the right to file a whistleblower complaint with OSHA if you believe your employer retaliated against you for exercising your rights as an employee under the whistleblower protection laws enforced by OSHA. In States with OSHA-approved State Plans, employees may file complaints under section 11(c) of the Occupational Safety and Health Act with Federal OSHA and with the State Plan under its equivalent statutory provision.

What to Expect During a Whistleblower Investigation

Filing a Complaint

An employee, or his or her representative, can file a whistleblower complaint with OSHA via mail, fax, telephone, in person, or online, against an employer for unlawful retaliation. During the investigation, the employee who files the complaint is referred to as "the Complainant," and the employer, against whom the complaint is filed, is referred to as "the Respondent." Neither side is required to retain an attorney, but if a party designates a representative, the designee will serve as the point of contact with OSHA.

It is imperative for the Complainant or his or her representative to provide OSHA with current contact information. Failure to do so may cause OSHA to conclude the investigation.

OSHA will interview the Complainant to obtain information about the alleged retaliation, and will determine whether the allegation is sufficient to initiate an investigation under one or more of the whistleblower protection statutes administered by OSHA. Regardless of the statute under which the complaint is filed, the conduct of the investigation is generally the same.

Investigative Process

If the allegation is sufficient to proceed with an investigation, the complaint will be assigned to an OSHA whistleblower Investigator who is a neutral fact-finder who does not represent either party. The investigator will notify the Complainant, Respondent, and appropriate federal partner agency that OSHA has opened an investigation.

The Complainant and the Respondent should keep any potential evidence regarding the circumstances of the allegations, including all pertinent emails, letters, notes, text messages, voicemails, phone logs, personnel files, contracts, work products, and meeting minutes.

OSHA will request that both parties provide each other with a copy of all submissions they have made to OSHA related to the complaint. Both the Complainant and the Respondent should provide contact information for witnesses who could support or refute the alleged retaliation.

OSHA will ask the Respondent to provide a written defense to the allegations, also known as a position statement. Both parties are expected to actively participate in the investigation and to respond to OSHA's requests. Both parties are also given an opportunity to rebut the opposing party's position.

Whistleblower investigations vary in length of time. The parties may settle the retaliation complaint at any point in the investigation either through OSHA's Alternative Dispute Resolution (ADR) program, with the assistance of the assigned investigator, or through their own negotiated settlement that OSHA approves.

Under certain statutes, the Complainant may "kick out" and file the retaliation complaint in federal district court if there is no final order and a specified time from the filing of the complaint with OSHA has passed (180 or 210 days depending on the statute).

Conclusion of the Investigation

At the conclusion of the investigation, the investigator will make a recommendation to his/her supervisor regarding whether the evidence provides reasonable cause to believe that the Respondent violated the specific statute in question. If the supervisor and management concur with the merit or dismissal recommendation, OSHA will issue a findings letter to both parties, which will include information about remedies (if appropriate) and the right to object and have the case heard by an administrative law judge, except in cases under section 11(c), AHERA, or ISCA. In those cases, Complainants may request review by OSHA's National Office of dismissal decisions. In merit section 11(c), AHERA, or ISCA cases, unless a settlement is reached, the Department of Labor would have to file a complaint in district court to remedy the retaliation.

> *"Not all anonymous accusers and whistleblowers have righteous motives. Some are out to advance their own careers and feather their own nests."*

Corrupt Whistleblowers Should Not Be Protected

Alan A. Cavaiola

In this viewpoint, Alan A. Cavaiola writes that while good whistleblowers provide a valuable service, not all of them have altruistic motives. Some are motivated purely by self-interest. Some self-described "whistleblowers" lie and falsify information in order to advance themselves or take others down. Cavaiola uses specific examples of false whistleblowing to support his argument that such people should not be protected by whistleblower laws. Alan A. Cavaiola is a professor in the department of psychological counseling at Monmouth University in New Jersey, where he is a member of the graduate faculty. Cavaiola has co-authored three books with Neil Lavender: Toxic Coworkers: How to Deal with Dysfunctional People on the Job, The One Way Relationship Workbook, *and* Impossible to Please.

"Beware the Whistleblower," by Alan A. Cavaiola, Psychology Today LLC, October 26, 2016. Reprinted by permission.

As you read, consider the following questions:

1. What happened during the Enron scandal, according to Cavaiola?

2. What suggestions does Cavaiola offer in order to separate truthful whistleblowers from corrupt ones?

3. How does Cavaiola use the example of New Jersey ex-governor Chris Christie to support his ideas?

What comes to mind when you hear the word, "whistleblower"? Usually, this term conjures up images of employees who put their jobs and livelihoods on the line in order to expose workplace improprieties like fraud or other abuses whether they be illegal, immoral or unethical. In one of my previous blogs, I wrote about having attended a lecture by Sherron Watkins, who was one of the primary whistleblowers in exposing the Enron scandal. It was incredible to hear how Ms. Watkins had gone from being among the inner circle at Enron, to then discovering how Enron execs were using fraudulent tactics to drive up the price of Enron stock and to manipulate the natural gas markets. Even worse was when these same executives had absconded with Enron employee retirement funds in order to cover up debts. When the house of cards collapsed, Enron went down hard and many within the Enron upper echelon faced prison time, while Enron employees (including Watkins) were left without jobs or pensions.

However, not all whistleblowers are alike. Take for example the work of Stieg Berge Matthiesen, Brita Bjørkelo and Ronald J. Burke (2011), who had written a work entitled: *Workplace Bullying as the Dark Side of Whistleblowing*. They provide a thorough description of both the altruistic whistleblower and those whistleblowers who are motivated by purely by self-interest. Terance Miethe (1999) points out that while some whistleblowers can be seen as altruistic, selfless individuals who take action at "extraordinary personal cost" others can best be described as "selfish and egotistical" (often described as "snitches", "rats", "moles", "finks" and "blabbermouths". It is important therefore to look at the motivations of whistleblowers. For example are they motivated by a sense of moral conscience in order to right some wrong or to bring corrective action to situations where corporations, organizations or individuals are acting in illegal, immoral or illegitimately? This type of whistleblower usually is acting altruistically for the greater good. However, what about situations where the "whistleblower" does not act based upon altruistic motives such as exposing corruption, fraud or wrongdoing but rather acts out of greed, revenge, or to increase the likelihood of advancing themselves up the corporate ladder? What about situations in which the "whistleblower" lies or creates false information in order to bring down a supervisor, CEO or fellow employee and may do so anonymously however, under existing whistleblower laws these individuals would also be protected from retaliation, in the same way that those who expose fraud or theft for moral or altruistic reasons are protected. Most of us have no problem with true whistleblowers being afforded protection under the law when their cause is just and good, but what about fraudulent whistleblowers who lie and falsify information to advance themselves? Isn't one of the Ten Commandments, "Thou Shalt Not Bear False Witness Against Thy Neighbor"? In other words, don't make up lies about other people, right?

In an actual case of fraudulent whistleblowing that we are personally aware of, a State government division director who had been appointed by the Governor of that state for her expertise and 20 years of experience in her profession was vilified by a group of sociopathic state bureaucrats who had been passed over for promotions. The director finally was forced to resign when she was accused of giving grants to "her friends", when in actuality, grant expansion was an acceptable practice among her predecessors. Plus every dollar of grant money spent was accounted for as it went to building projects and program service expansion. You can hopefully see from this example why many experts want no part of state or federal government because of the types of backbiting that we briefly describe above, along with red tape that prevents committed individuals from being able to do the right thing and actually get things done. Instead what most bureaucrats learn is how to play the game. What makes matters even worse is when "outsiders" to state or federal government are appointed to positions of authority without any staff to support them. Usually they don't last long and the message they come away with is "experts need not apply".

So what can we learn from this "whistleblower" story? First, not all whistleblowers are courageous, moral and altruistic like Sherron Watkins or the chemist, Jeff Wigand who exposed the tobacco industry's lies to the public regarding the true harm of cigarette smoking. Not all anonymous accusers and whistleblowers have righteous motives. Some are out to advance their own careers and feather their own nests. When determining which is which, there are two suggestions: 1) determine who benefits from the whistleblower's taking action and 2) follow the money…i.e. who gains monetarily.

To all you sociopaths-in-training out there, if you want to get rid of your boss, a co-worker or even a CEO, make up lies about them and sit back and watch the fireworks. Say they're having sex with sheep or something equally as outrageous because by the time the dust settles and your boss or supervisor is exonerated, there will still be those who believe everything they read in the newspaper and will still be thinking, "maybe my boss was having sex with sheep". Take for example the current governor of New Jersey, Chris Christie. There have been two major instances where Christie had been accused of improprieties. The first and most recent is the Bridge Gate scandal, which is just beginning to gain some traction. Some say that Bridge Gate may have been a major factor why Christie was not chosen as Trump's running mate. The other involved a story broken by the *New York Times* in 2012 which alleged Christie's ties to multi-million dollar contracts being awarded to state-funded halfway houses for individuals coming out of states prisons. The Times reported that many of these halfway houses were poorly supervised and it was common for halfway house residents to leave prior to serving their time. In one such instance, one of these ex-cons, David Goodell, who took off from these poorly run halfway house, subsequently killed an ex-girlfriend. (Sounds similar to the Willy Horton case that plagued presidential candidate Michael Dukakis' campaign?) But despite a multi-page story in the *New York Times* by reporter Sam Dolnick, the accusations make against Christie never gained traction. Many to this day, still question why?

So here's something to think about. Why do some actual instances of impropriety, fraud or corruption reported by whistleblowers never result in any substantive changes (as in the case of Governor Christie) while in other instances false accusations made by anonymous whistleblowers can result in qualified people losing their jobs. This would make an interesting study to look at instances where whistleblower accusations get traction where in other instances they fall by the wayside.

References

Toxic Coworkers: How to Deal With Dysfunctional People on the Job. A. Cavaiola and N. Lavender.

Babiak, P. & Hare, R. D. (2006). Snakes in Suits: When Psychopaths Go to Work. New York: Harper Collins.

Dolnick, Sam (2012, June 16). As escapees stream out, a penal business thrives. New York Times. article continues after advertisement

Krugman, Paul (2012, June 21). Prisons, privatization and patronage. New York Times.

Mattiesen, S. B., Bjorkelo, B., & Burke, R. J. (2011). Workplace bullying as the dark side of

Whistleblowing. In S. Einarsen, H. Hoel, Zapf, D. & Cooper, C.L.(Eds.) Bullying and

Harassment in the Workplace.2nd ed Boca Raton, FL: CRC Press/Taylor & Francis Group (pp 301-324).

Miethe, T. D. (1999). Whistleblowing at work: Tough choices in exposing fraud, waste andabuse on the job. Boulder, CO: Westview Press.

Periodical and Internet Sources Bibliography

The following articles have been selected to supplement the diverse views presented in this chapter.

John J. Carney and Alexandra Karambelas, "When a Whistleblower Is Wrong—Time for a Proactive Defense," Bloomberg Law, January 6, 2022. https://news.bloomberglaw.com/securities-law/when-a-whistleblower-is-wrong-time-for-a-proactive-defense.

Louis Clark and Brian McLaren, "Potential whistleblowers deserve more support. Their moral choices protect our democracy," *USA Today*, February 13, 2021. https://www.usatoday.com/story/opinion/2021/02/13/whistleblowers-protect-democracy-we-must-protect-them-column/4406728001/.

Sarah Cords, "Why Whistleblowers Need More Protection," the *Progressive*. February 11, 2021. https://progressive.org/latest/whistleblowers-need-more-protection-cords-210211/.

Marissel Descalzo, "Employers Fight Back Against Whistleblowers," Tache, Bronis and Descalzo, P. A., July 2, 2014. https://tachebronis.com/employers-fight-back-against-whistleblowers/.

Embroker Team, "Whistleblower Retaliation: Risks Both Sides Need to Know," Embroker, September 7, 2022. https://www.embroker.com/blog/whistleblower-retaliation-risks/.

Lee Fang, "Pfizer Is Lobbying to Thwart Whistleblowers from Exposing Corporate Fraud," the *Intercept*, November 29, 2021. https://theintercept.com/2021/11/29/pfizer-whistleblower-reform-corporate-fraud.

Jean-Philippe Foegle, "Endorsing Whistleblowing as a Democratic Accountability Mechanism: Benefits of a Human-Rights Based Approach to Whistleblower Protection," United Nations Human Rights Office of the High Commissioner, June 2015. https://www.ohchr.org/sites/default/files/Documents/Issues/Opinion/Protection/JeanPhilippeFoegle.pdf.

Dana Gold, "Whistleblowers Risk Everything—Lawmakers Must Protect Them," Government Executive, October 28, 2021. https://www.govexec.com/oversight/2021/10/whistleblowers-risk-everythinglawmakers-must-protect-them/186441/.

Karen Graham, "Op-Ed: How Safe Are Whistleblowers? A Look at Canada and the U.S.," Digital Journal, November 17, 2019. https://www.digitaljournal.com/world/op-ed-how-safe-are-whistleblowers-a-look-at-canada-and-the-usa/article/561927#ixzz7nGeTI1na.

Lisa Guerin, "Wrongful Termination: RetaliationWhistleblowing," NOLO. https://www.nolo.com/legal-encyclopedia/wrongful-termination-retaliation-whistleblowing.html.

Michael Johnson, "Opinion: Frances Haugen Exposed a Gaping Hole in Whistleblower Protection," *Politico*, November 23, 2021. https://www.politico.com/news/magazine/2021/11/23/whistleblower-laws-haugen-facebook-johnson-blue-shield-523204.

D. Robert MacDougall, "Whistleblowing: Don't Encourage It, Prevent It," *International Journal of Health Policy and Management,* March 2016. https://www.ncbi.nlm.nih.gov/pmc/articles/PMC4770925/.

Frederik Obermaier and Bastian Obermayer, "Op-Ed: Whistleblowers Are Vital to Democracy. We Need to Better Protect Them," *Los Angeles Times.* April 9, 2018. https://www.latimes.com/opinion/op-ed/la-oe-obermaier-obermayer-whistleblowers-20180409-story.html.

Allison Stanger, "Why America Needs Whistle-Blowers," the *New York Times*, October 6, 2019. https://www.nytimes.com/2019/10/06/opinion/trump-whistleblower.html.

Stephen Still, "A Public Concern: Protecting Whistleblowers Under the First Amendment," *Fordham Law Review*, March 2020. http://fordhamlawreview.org/wp-content/uploads/2020/03/Still_March_N_9.pdf.

OPPOSING
VIEWPOINTS®
SERIES

Should Police Officers Break the Code of Silence and Blow the Whistle?

Chapter Preface

Early in director Sidney Lumet's 1973 film version of a whistleblower cop's life, *Serpico*, two policemen are talking at the precinct. "Guess who got shot?... Serpico," the first cop says. "Think a cop did it?" the other asks. "I know six cops said they'd like to," is the reply. That scene is fictionalized, but the story is real.

Frank Serpico, a renegade cop who could not abide the rampant corruption in the New York City Police Department of the early 1970s, is shot in the face as a reward for breaking the police code of silence. Juxtaposed with scenes of emergency room doctors and nurses working on Serpico is a flashback to his police academy graduation ceremony. The speaker tells the new officers that "Every day, your life will be on the line. And also your character. You'll need integrity, courage, honesty, compassion, courtesy, perseverance, and patience." Serpico is an officer who actually possesses these traits…and it lands him in the hospital.

Serpico, produced in 1973, is perhaps the most famous cinematic portrayal of a whistleblower cop, and the repercussions that occur when he pushes too hard against corruption. It is based on the true story of Frank Serpico, who, along with Sergeant David Durk, bucked the system. Their revelations led to the creation of the Commission to Investigate Alleged Police Corruption (also known as the Knapp Commission), a five-member panel that ultimately concluded that New York City's police department was home to widespread and systematic corruption.

But Serpico's efforts, noble as they were, did not put an end to the police code of silence in New York City or anywhere else. The code of silence—which is also known as the blue wall of silence, the blue code, and the blue shield—persists. The terms are used to denote the supposed informal code of silence among police officers in the United States to not report on a colleague's mistakes, misconduct, or crimes, especially those related to police brutality. Officers who do inform on their corrupt colleagues often learn that it is far better to keep one's mouth closed, especially if a cop wants to hold onto their job, paycheck, and pension. Promotions are usually out of the question.

As Casey J. Bastian writes,

> To those behind this thin blue line, their most dangerous enemy is the upright cop: the whistleblower. To them, this is "snitching," which is a mortal sin in any criminal or corrupt organization. An act of betrayal and treason that must be punished. Those willing to violate this code, to pierce this "blue wall of silence," must be removed through any available means. If this retribution destroys the life of an otherwise solid cop, so be it.[1]

When Serpico attempts to report police corruption to the higher ups, he is told to "forget it." The scene may be fictionalized, but the message is historically accurate. Police who blow the whistle are denigrated by their colleagues as "rats," ostracized, and harassed. They will be "alone on the streets," meaning that other officers will no longer have their backs.

Serpico was shot in 1971. Over 50 years later, observers may well wonder what has changed. Police corruption may not be as systematic and widespread as it was in the 1960s, but the code of silence seems as strong as ever. Every so often there are cracks in the wall, such as in the case of George Floyd, who was murdered in Minnesota by officer Derek Chauvin in 2020. At trial, three officers testified against him. But the case was such a blatant example of police brutality that the cruelty and criminality could not be ignored, even by Chauvin's colleagues. In thousands of other cases across the country, the blue wall of silence is there to ensure that cops get away with behavior similar to that for which they put other citizens in prison.

Notes

1. Casey J. Bastien, "The Blue Wall of Silence: Law Enforcement Whistleblowers Face Severe Retaliation," *Criminal Legal New*, September 15, 2022. https://www.criminallegalnews.org/news/2022/sep/15/blue-wall-silence-law-enforcement-whistleblowers-face-severe-retaliation/.

> *"Yes, we need major police reform now all across the United States of America. The entire United States, a constitutional, democratic republic, needs urgent reform now and desperately so."*

Corrupt Police Departments Are in Desperate Need of an Overhaul

William Dudley Bass

In this viewpoint, William Dudley Bass writes that the murder of George Floyd by a police officer in 2020 is an indication that police departments need to be scrutinized and overhauled. Bass suggests three specific ways in which police departments can be improved: democratic community oversight, defunding and reallocation of resources, and demilitarization. He describes the concept of "defunding" the police, which he then explains is not the same as abolishing the police. As police brutality and the murder of citizens by police has increased, Bass writes, deep structural transformation of our local and global systems are needed, and not merely changes and reforms. William Dudley Bass is a blogger and freelance writer living in Seattle, Washington.

"The Killing of George Floyd, Black Lives Matter Right Now, and Overhaul the Police Immediately," William Dudley Bass, June 1, 2020. Reprinted by permission.

As you read, consider the following questions:

1. How does Bass differentiate defunding the police from abolishing the police?
2. Why does Bass refer to officers' killing of citizens as "lynchings"?
3. How does Bass place responsibility on American politicians and policies for the continued mistreatment of marginalized citizens in the U.S.?

George Perry Floyd, a Black American, was pulled out into the street, lynched, and murdered at age 46 by four police officers in Minneapolis, Minnesota. His killers were three White or European American cops and one Asian American cop. Mr. Floyd's criminal background is not relevant here. The man had served his time in prison and served his Houston, Texas, community for years as a volunteer. He finally moved north into the Upper Midwest to start life anew. There wasn't one single thing George Floyd did or was alleged to have done that warranted his slow, brutal death by a man who taunted him at times with what sounded like sadistic glee.

Yes, we need major police reform now all across the United States of America. The entire United States, a constitutional, democratic republic, needs urgent reform now and desperately so. We must not abolish our police forces, but instead reform or replace them immediately in three primary areas.

First, we need community oversight that is also democratic and transparent. Every city, town, parish, tribal reservation, and county jurisdiction, if they have not yet done so must shift to democratic community oversight. This may include re-creating the role of police as defacto paramilitary enforcers to instead become community servants. Cops must live in the jurisdictions they work in as part of belonging to the community.

Second, defund, not abolish, the police. To implement what "Defund the Police!" actually means, i.e. to review funding and reallocate police resources to non-police agencies and departments such as health care, dealing with addiction, homelessness, affordable housing, public sanitation, public infrastructure, etc. Doing so will allow for a stripped down, leaner community-based police force more focused and thus more efficient on policing, i.e. to serve and protect the public. Indeed, police reform may require increasing the number of police to actually serve and protect the public while non-police agencies focus on non-police public health, housing, infrastructure, and other social services.

Third, demilitarize the police. Yes, we must move to demilitarize the police and stop the flow of military hardware from the Armed Forces to the cops. Yes, SWAT teams for certain jurisdictions, of course, but how many, where, and for whom? Reviewing the relationships between local law enforcement and the FBI, ATF, ICE, Homeland Security, etc., is a necessary aspect of such purview.

So, three reforms: democratic community oversight, defunding and reallocation of resources, and demilitarization.

There's one more reform, one perhaps more serious than the other three and one that certainly presents difficult challenges: reports and allegations of police brutality shall be reviewed with serious efforts to break apart the insidious and unethical Police Code of Silence. This code of silence corrupts the Thin Blue Line between cops and their communities, allows for both corruption and brutality to go unchecked. Criminality and division results. Criminals, including crooked and abusive cops, must be brought to justice. Securing and upholding our individual liberties demand we all hold each other and our public servants accountable. Our singular freedoms work only if we also acknowledge and uphold our social responsibilities. One large city, Camden, New Jersey, abolished its police department largely in part to exorcise entrenched, endemic police corruption and brutality.

The latest round of killings of Black Americans by police are clearly acts of murder. Indeed, they are lynchings, abusive and hateful lynchings by those sworn to serve and protect. These murders have convulsed our country again. First Ahmaud Arbery was killed in Brunswick, Georgia on the 23rd of February this year. [Local law enforcement was criticized for not taking the investigation seriously and failing to make an arrest for two months after the murder.] Then Breonna Taylor was killed in a fusillade of bullets in Louisville, Kentucky on the 23rd of March. The sadistic, slow, asphyxiation of George Floyd on the 25th of May blew open a nation already torn apart. The deaths and injuries kept coming. They keep on coming, too. Tony McDade, a Black transgender man, was shot dead by cops in Tallahassee, Florida, on the 29 of

CAN THE CODE OF SILENCE BE BROKEN?

The mayor's speech Wednesday addressed what is sometimes called the "blue code of silence"—officers lying to cover for other officers.

CBS 2's Mai Martinez reports that code of silence was under discussion at a meeting held by the Chicago Urban League.

About 300 people attended the forum. Many say the mayor addressing the code of silence among officers is a good start, but they question whether he or anyone can actually end it.

It might be surprising to hear the mayor address it publicly, but the code is no secret to any officer.

"It's gone on for so long, as long as I know, and I was a police officer beginning over 30 years ago," said retired Chicago Police Officer Lorenzo Davis.

For nearly seven years, Davis also served as a supervising investigator for the Independent Police Review Authority, the agency tasked with investigating complaints against CPD officers.

When asked how often a cover-up seemed to be happening, Davis said cover-ups, "seemed to be happening routinely with excessive force cases and police involved shooting cases."

That's no surprise to Craig Futterman, a University of Chicago law professor who helped to get the Laquan McDonald dash cam video released. He says the code destroys trust in the police, but some officers feel they have no choice.

"You don't rat on a fellow police officers or else," Futterman said. "That's the end of your career, could be the end of your life."

continued on next page

> Futterman says the mayor addressing the issue is a good start, but only action can end the code.
>
> "You protect officers that come forward," Futterman said. "Anyone retaliates against them in any way shape or form, they're fired."
>
> But Lakeisha Miller who attended the Urban League forum with her 10-year-old son says holding the police accountable is only one part of the solution.
>
> The code of silence isn't just with the Police Department," she said. "I feel that the leadership in the city of Chicago, they all need to break their code of silence."
>
> Public outrage over the Laquan McDonald shooting is driving these calls for more police accountability, but we should note, it was a member of law enforcement who broke the code of silence that started the ball rolling on the fight to get that dash cam video released.
>
> **"Can Police Officers' Code of Silence Be Broken?" by Mai Martinez, CBS Chicago, December 9, 2015.**

May, 2020. David McAtee of Louisville, Kentucky, known as Yaya the BBQ Man, was shot dead by cops on the 1st of June 2020. The list keeps growing.

These terrifying murders pushed a nation already traumatized by the COVID-19 pandemic, an economic collapse, climate change, asteroids nearly every other weekend, endless wars and threats of world war, impeachment proceedings, mass extinction, and the cruel and stupid behavior of one jerk of a U.S. president gone over the edge. Donald Trump won the American presidency by manipulating and intimidating the Electoral College after losing the popular vote to Hillary Clinton by nearly three million people. This shamefully, indeed dangerously incompetent buffoon revels in threats of civil war and labels peaceful protesters all "looters" and "thugs" to be walled out and shot at. Trump called the nations many Black and Hispanic immigrants and refugees are from "sh*thole countries," but calls Alt-Right White Supremacists "very fine people." He ignores the U.S. Constitution, teases his Red-hatted goons to punch out his opponents, and calls for the police to stop being "nice" when making arrests and even go rough people up.

This didn't even start with the cops killing our fellow citizens listed above earlier this year. There was Eric Garner on 17 July 2014 in New York City. Michael Brown on the 9th of August 2014 in Ferguson, Missouri. Freddie Gray in Baltimore, Maryland on 19 April 2015.

Remember Trayvon Martin? Shot dead wearing a hoodie in Sanford, Florida? On the 26th of February 2012? Black Lives Matter sprung up out of this in 2013 with demonstrations and riots across the country lasting well into 2016 and 2017.

This is part of a larger cycle of civil unrest and low-level domestic warfare, too, beginning with the Wisconsin Insurrection of February–June 2011. That was followed by the Occupy Wall Street revolt in September 2011 that morphed into Occupy Earth/ Occupy Everywhere and eventually became what we called the Occupy Movement of 2011-2016. There was the Water Protectors Movement galvanized by the Dakota Access Pipeline (DAPL) protests springing up on the Standing Rock Indian Reservation in April 2016 and spread across the U.S. well into February 2017.

These events dovetailed with the chaotic election campaign of 2016 resulting in the winning of the American Presidency by Donald Trump, a corrupt, White business tycoon from New York in 2017. His election was followed by waves of protests and marches continuing to this day in 2020. Many of the anti-Trump Resistance actions were peaceful, but violence erupted and grew as Trump egged on his followers. The so-called Alt-Right came out in force on the Far Right and was sometimes challenged by Antifa on the Far Left. Violent fights and skirmishes broke out between them and between them and the police and other demonstrators. These fights flared from Washington, D.C., to Portland, Oregon, to Sacramento, California, to Charlottesville, Virginia.

There was a large uptick in hate crimes, especially on the Far Right by various White Supremacist groups. This was also against a background of right-wing militia revolts such as the ones led by the Bundy family and their allies in Nevada (2014) and in Oregon (2016), and growing, ugly outbursts of mass shootings and gun massacres that seem to grind on and on. This low-level war of sorts is waged on multiple fronts including cyberspace, mainstream mass media, social media, financial institutions and markets, and within divided government institutions, fracturing political parties, and angry communities.

What must recognize Americans are embroiled in a form of LIC or Low-Intensity Conflict, a type of intermittent, civil war among and between disorganized yet highly networked groups and individuals. We all need deep, structural transformation of our local and global systems, not merely changes and reforms. To do so, however, we as a species must find ways to accept what is so before we can move to change what we seek to change. We must learn to work together in spite of what divides us and find common ground. The extremists on the Far Right and the Far Left as well as the fanatics among our many religions will fight these moves. Love 'em and leave 'em, I say.

We must find ways to practice the practices of compassion, lovingkindness, forgiveness, flexibility, courage, love, and the backbone to stand firm in the face of violence, hatred, and bigotry to fight for justice. We must find our capacity for empathy and respect. And know when to let go and move forward. If others call this approach "radical," let them, for being radical simply means going back to the roots of something, i.e. something already rooted.

At different times in our nation's history many have spoken up for justice, representation, and, indeed, recognizance—to simply be seen, and, yes, sadly, resorting to violence when they don't feel seen as human beings. Yes, people have a need to be seen, to be recognized, and to be listened to, not just heard. When you say, "I hear you," did you actually listen?

The list is long: homeless people, Native Americans, Latinx, women, Blacks, Asians, working class folks, immigrants, children, the elderly, the disabled, veterans, those with chronic illnesses of all kinds, people from different religions and subcultures, people from across the spectrum of different sexual, gender, and relationship identities, on and on, as, gosh, the list of our diversity is so very rich. Now Black human beings are rising up, again, with or without their allies, to demand the rest of us understand Black Lives Matter!

Yes, we often don't know the best words or actions. We mess up and will mess up again. Life is messy! Then let's root ourselves deeper in our messes. Aye, root ourselves deep into the dirt, deep into the soil, root ourselves deeper into our network of communities. Let's find new ways to work together. Again, if this is radical, then embrace this. Embrace your roots. Let's embrace our roots together! Why do we make doing so, so difficult?

Yes, we live during a time where so many overlapping crises and wicked problems converge and overwhelm us. Our world feels apocalyptic. Just know all these things shall pass. We are, however, at choice as what steps we take to respond to our communal challenges. We are at choice as what steps we choose to take as we move forward. We are all at choice as to how we show up as we move thru our lives.

Right now, however, we must not just change and reform our police but transform our communities including our police. If you wanna all hold hands and sing "Kumbaya" around the campfire together as One People, well, we're all gotta work and work damn hard to get there. Violence often appears the easiest way out, doesn't it? Yet resorting to violence, resorting to what should be the last resort usually makes every problem much more difficult to resolve.

> *"I've always spoke up against things*
> *I thought was wrong within the*
> *department. But like you said, this*
> *culture right now, a lot of officers*
> *don't feel as though they can speak*
> *up because there's no real, true*
> *mechanism that protects us from*
> *retaliation from our superiors."*

There Are Consequences When Officers Speak Up

Michel Martin

In this viewpoint, Michel Martin interviews Sergeant Isaac Lambert and former officer Lorenzo Davis, who discuss the problems associated with breaking the police code of silence. Both men had issues with the way reports were written to cover up malpractice or other inappropriate actions by Chicago police officers. Both men were not supported by their superiors. Lambert states that he was not "demoted," but he was removed from his role as a detective and put back on patrol. Davis was fired from a police review board. The men believe that the department has retaliated against them for refusing to tell untruths about police-citizen interactions. National Public Radio (NPR) is an independent, nonprofit media organization that was founded on a mission to create a more informed public. Michel Martin is a correspondent for NPR.

As you read, consider the following questions:

1. What incident caused Lorenzo Davis to be removed from a police review board?
2. What incident caused Isaac Lambert to be removed from his position as a detective?
3. According to Lambert and Davis, why does the police code of silence persist?

NPR's Michel Martin speaks to Chicago police Sgt. Isaac Lambert and former Chicago officer Lorenzo Davis about the consequences they faced speaking out against fellow officers and police misconduct.

MICHEL MARTIN, HOST: The police killing of George Floyd has brought on a national reckoning about policing in America, especially about police brutality and why it persists. One key question—if abuses are committed by a few bad apples, as some have called the officers involved, why don't other officers speak up or intervene to stop those abuses?

To gain some insight on this, we've called two men who say they have felt the consequences of speaking out in that way. Lorenzo Davis is a former Chicago police officer who won a $2.8 million judgment after he was fired from a now-defunct police review board. He was serving as a civilian member then. He says he was fired for refusing to change his findings about police misconduct. And a court evidently agreed.

Mr. Davis, thanks for joining us.

LORENZO DAVIS: Oh, thank you. Glad to be here.

MARTIN: Also with us is Sergeant Ike Lambert. He is a former detective and current patrol officer in Chicago who says he was retaliated against when he refused to sign off on a police report that he says was not true.

Sergeant Lambert, thank you so much for joining us as well.

IKE LAMBERT: Thank you for having me.

MARTIN: I mean—and I especially appreciate both of you speaking about events that have to have been painful for you. And I'm going to start with you, Sergeant Lambert. And I do want to mention that your lawsuit is still pending. But it stems from an incident in August 2017 when an off-duty Chicago police officer shot an unarmed 18-year-old. And you said that the initial police report was inaccurate, and so you refused to sign off. You know, what happened then? I mean, when did you start to feel that you were, in effect, going to be retaliated against?

LAMBERT: Well, basically, after a year or so, when the report and its investigation remained dormant, a FOIA request was submitted to the city of Chicago, which prompted action by my police department. (Unintelligible) Doing some things I thought were just not just in terms of the way we were categorizing that kid as offender and officer as a victim. I didn't agree with it.

MARTIN: How long had you been on the force by the time this happened?

LAMBERT: Twenty-four years.

MARTIN: And I was just wondering—if you hadn't been on for that long and had the seniority that you have, do you think that you would have reacted the same way? Do you think you would have stood your ground, as it were?

LAMBERT: I've always spoke up against things I thought was wrong within the department. But like you said, this culture right now, a lot of officers don't feel as though they can speak up because there's no real, true mechanism that protects us from retaliation from our superiors.

Unfortunately, right now, I'm a perfect example of that. I'm living proof that, you know, if you speak out and it's not what the department wants you to conform to, you'll be punished. Or they'll take action against you, and you really have no recourse unless you're strong enough to stand out there on the ledge. And a lot of people won't back you. They'll leave you out there for yourself, so that's—it's different.

MARTIN: So if you just describe, like, what happened—I mean, you had been a detective. What happened—that you were, in essence, demoted?

LAMBERT: I wasn't demoted. I was given an unfavorable position. I was put back in patrol. Working in the detective division is considered a prime position in the department. And when you get dumped back to the streets, it's different. You know, it happened four days after I didn't want to approve this report but I was made to. I'm dumped midweek.

MARTIN: And what about you, Mr. Davis? Talk to me about your situation. I mean, you joined the police review board after a career with the Chicago Police Department. You're also a licensed attorney. Why did you want to join that board?

DAVIS: I was interested in what I was reading in the daily newspapers about officer-involved shootings. I did not recall it being so many when I was—the 23 years that I was a police officer. So I was interested in finding out exactly what was going on in the city of Chicago, my city. And I began to find that there was a lot of misconduct that was being committed, and police officers were not being held accountable for it.

MARTIN: When did you realize, though—when did you start to believe that your evaluation of events was not appreciated? Let me just put it that way.

DAVIS: Actually, when the administration of that agency changed. A chief administrator came in, a new one, who was a retired DEA agent—had a police—you might say a policing background. And he was also a member of the federal Fraternal Order of Police. It was at that time that my reports were being rejected.

MARTIN: And was it—was anything ever said to you? I mean, did he ever say to you, this isn't the way it's going to be or anything like that? Like, how did—was it just that your reports were never accepted?

DAVIS: He said to me that I appeared to be biased against police officers. He ordered me to change them, and I would not do it. I said, in order to change my findings, what I would have to do is change the evidence and witness statements and the like. And that would be unlawful, actually.

MARTIN: Can I ask each of you—why does this persist? I mean, I know maybe to you, it's a ridiculous question because you've lived it every day. But a lot of people want to know—why does this persist? You know, what is it that allows this to continue? So I don't know—Mr. Davis, you want to start?

DAVIS: Now, the situation persists, I think, because of the confidentiality that exists within the organization. And when you have that much confidentiality, you have no transparency.

MARTIN: What do you think, Sergeant Lambert? Like, what's your take on why this persists?

LAMBERT: I think some more important factors to me—the accountability of the investigations and meaning that we have an investigation of a bad police officer, it should be done in a manner that doesn't take three to four years. It should be dealt with swiftly by the supervisors, whoever sees to that. But I think the problem with a lot of people on our job is their moral compass. Sometimes it's integrity and being a professional when you do your job.

I mean, we're talking about things that just shouldn't happen. So why do they happen? Because we don't correct them. We don't discipline. We don't do what needs to be done. You know, like I say, you have so many different cliques, so many different biases from people. But at the same time, that shouldn't matter if you just do your job.

MARTIN: Ike Lambert is a sergeant with the Chicago Police Department.

Sergeant Lambert, thank you for joining us.

LAMBERT: Thank you for having me.

MARTIN: Lorenzo Davis is an attorney and former supervising investigator of Chicago's Independent Police Review Authority.

Mr. Davis, thank you so much for joining us as well.

DAVIS: And thank you for having me on.

MARTIN: And we should say we reached out to the Chicago Police Department for comment. We haven't received a response yet.

> *"Whistleblowers aren't just seen as stabbing other officers in the back, they're almost inevitably seen as a potential physical threat to every officer."*

Police Whistleblowers Put Themselves in Jeopardy

Isidoro Rodriguez

In this viewpoint, Isidoro Rodriguez considers the longstanding and ingrained police code of silence in the wake of the George Floyd murder by policeman Derek Chauvin. In a profession where colleagues work closely with each other, where intense and dangerous situations can be common, and where their very lives are sometimes threatened, police officers feel the need to stick together against the citizenry and even against the higher-ups in their departments. They are reluctant to report misconduct, and protecting each other is an expectation. Rodriguez states that stronger, more impactful leadership in police departments would help alleviate the problem, but such leadership is not common. According to Rodriguez, there are roughly 18,000 state, county, and local law enforcement agencies in the United States today. With no national standards, departments come up with their own rules. Isidoro Rodriguez is a contributing writer for the Crime Report.

"The Plight of the Police Whistleblower," by Isidoro Rodriguez, The Crime Report, June 18, 2020. Reprinted by permission. This article was originally published in The Crime Report: https://thecrimereport.org/2020/06/18/the-plight-of-the-police-whistleblower/.

As you read, consider the following questions:

1. How does the type of work that police do encourage the code of silence?
2. What perks was Shannon Spalding offered to keep her quiet?
3. How did the Supreme Court ruling in the case of *Garcetti v. Ceballos* affect police whistleblowers?

E ven as municipal and state officials around the country react to the killing of George Floyd with measures aimed at curbing police misconduct, members of the criminal justice community warn that little will change unless officers feel safe enough to expose wrongdoing in their ranks.

Interviews with policing experts and former cops underlined the strength of a systemic police "culture of silence" that protects and supports bad officers, ignores officers in distress, and actively prevents good officers from speaking out as "whistleblowers" and demanding reform.

"There is tremendous pressure in policing, a cultural pressure, to not expose fellow officers to either professional or physical threats," Seth Stoughton, an associate professor of law at the University of South Carolina School of Law, and a former Tallahassee, Fl., police officer, told The Crime Report.

"[Reporting] on other cops is, in some sense, a betrayal of that cultural imperative to support and protect each other."

Police officers are an extremely insular group. They work closely with one another in what can often be a confrontational, adversarial and legitimately dangerous work environment. In a job where the man or woman next to you could be responsible for saving your life, it can be very difficult, if not impossible, to separate the character of someone who chooses to report misconduct from that of someone who will leave them in the lurch when their life is at risk.

"Whistleblowers aren't just seen as stabbing other officers in the back, they're almost inevitably seen as a potential physical threat to every officer," said Stoughton.

And that perceived threat is often met with retaliation. One of the most well-known examples is Frank Serpico, a former New York Police Department detective whose accusation of widespread corruption in the department during the late 1960s nearly cost him his life—and formed the plot of a gripping Hollywood film released in 1973.

But more than half a century later, police whistleblowers are still at risk.

Modern-day Serpicos risk stalled careers, ostracism from their colleagues, hostility from their superiors—and worse.

After reporting an instance of officer brutality in 2011, former Baltimore police officer Joe Crystal was actively harassed for the next two years by fellow officers who labeled him a rat, threatened his career, refused to help him, and placed a dead rat on the windshield of his car outside of his home.

At times, when Crystal called for backup while pursuing suspects on the job, he would be ignored.

In 2018, a female former Spokane, Wa., police officer who accused a male colleague of sexual assault reported being immediately ostracized by her fellow officers, facing open hostility in the workplace, and being avoided by people who, before her complaint, she had considered friends.

In both cases, the officers eventually left the force. Crystal had to leave the state.

"Because officers rely on each other so much, once an officer has blown the whistle or complained about a colleague, now that trust that had to exist between them either doesn't exist anymore or has been weakened," said Stoughton.

"It puts a target on their back."

Officers who decide to report misconduct are often penalized by their superiors as well.

In 2019, Chicago police officer Sgt. Isaac Lambert filed a lawsuit against his department for allegedly retaliating against him after he refused to change a police report regarding the shooting of an unarmed, autistic teen. He claimed they immediately transferred him from the department's detective division to a shift in the patrol division.

In 2017, the police department in McFarland, Ca., settled a lawsuit with two officers who claimed they were demoted and fired respectively after informing the FBI of their department's attempts to quash a warrant and protect the son of a city councilman suspected of being in possession of a stolen firearm.

"When officers challenge things or say things are unfair or not right, it's looked at as if the officer is challenging the chief's authority," said Stan Mason, host of the radio program "Behind The Blue Curtain", in an interview with TCR.

"The indoctrination is almost like the military."

A 25-year veteran of the Waco, Tx., Police Department, Mason argues that too often good officers enter departments where any misconduct they identify has most likely already become an unwritten policy that superiors and fellow officers would much rather sweep under the rug than actively address.

"It's easier to get rid of that person, or to bad-mouth that person, than it is to objectively look at their complaint and say whether it has merit or not," said Mason.

In a 2018 study examining how Swedish police officers learn and reproduce informal norms that condition the conversational and working climates of their organization, roughly 100 officers revealed the existence of two dominant narratives in their department: that sanctions will follow if officers voice their opinions, and that one's behavior must be adjusted if the ceiling of opportunity is to remain high.

The study further revealed that this culture is shared on a hierarchical level, with supervisors teaching trainees the culture of retaliation by retelling their own experiences with it and thereby granting it greater legitimacy, and that the discourse of a "low ceiling" of opportunity for those who speak up works performatively, constituting a plausible truth that few dare to question or challenge.

The benefits of staying silent are made clear in unsubtle ways, said Mason.

"Whether it's getting the vacation schedule before the next guy, getting to pick days off for the next year, getting to go to day shift, or this promotion or that promotion, of course they're going to keep toeing that line that got them there," he said.

The Rewards of 'Playing Ball'

The culture of keeping your head down and your mouth shut to get ahead was one of the first things Shannon Spalding learned when she joined the Chicago Police Department (CPD).

"What I learned very quickly is that if you play ball you go far, and if you don't you won't," said Spalding, who is no longer with the department.

An undercover narcotics officer working the neighborhoods of Chicago's South Side, Spalding spent five years working on a joint FBI/CPD internal affairs investigation that uncovered a massive criminal enterprise within the department.

A lawsuit that she later filed forced then-Mayor Rahm Emanuel to publicly admit that the CPD had protected crooked cops from justice, the first time in city history a powerful politician had ever publicly acknowledged the code of silence and the lives it destroys.

However, when she first made the decision to expose this corruption, Spalding says she was offered a way out that would have supposedly benefited everyone.

"I was promised that if I shut my mouth I would be made: new car, a work-from-home position, an insane amount of money, never having to show up for work. Just ride my time out and go away quietly," Spalding recalled.

This type of ethical erosion creates a lower standard for police behavior in a department where officers become numb to any of the varying degrees of misconduct they witness.

"You have officers inside the departments who see things that they know are inherently wrong, but if you say something you're told to mind your business," said Mason.

"How do you walk around in a department with 500 people who won't speak to you? How do you know they're not going to put something in your locker or your car and say we just ran the dogs around and they alerted on your car?"

Us vs. Them

According to a 2017 examination of police culture and work stress for Introduction To Policing, a police training textbook authored in part by former and current police officers, this perpetuated culture of silence creates an "us-vs.-them" mentality between superiors and their rank and file officers, who see themselves as members of a minority who have to take care of themselves.

Administrators are seen as dangerous outsiders who are both professionally and personally threatening.

"There is an institutional problem that does not encourage open communication," said Peter Moskos, an associate professor in the Department of Law, Police Science, and Criminal Justice Administration at John Jay College of Criminal Justice.

"It's a chain of command issue. You can never trust people two ranks above you because you're not supposed to deal with them."

A former Baltimore City Police officer, Moskos pointed out that many departments are often stuck paralyzed by fear, with seemingly no real way of telling what superiors might do if someone were to speak up.

"More likely, you send something up the chain of command and you never hear anything," said Moskos. "It disappears somewhere."

Moskos continued: "But what if they want to cover it up because they don't want the hassle? Should you be telling your boss how to do their job? Are they willing to throw people under the bus? You just don't know."

Uncertainty about how their complaints would be received can lead officers to make a variety of choices that at any time could endanger themselves and others.

A 2017 survey conducted by the Pew Research Center presented roughly 7,000 police officers around the country with a scenario in which an on-duty officer discovers a fellow officer who has been driving while intoxicated and gone into a ditch.

Instead of reporting the accident and offense, he drives the intoxicated officer home. In response to this scenario, 53 percent of the officers surveyed said that most officers in their department would not report the officer who covered up for his colleague. A quarter said only a few (22%) or none (5%) of their peers would report the cover-up.

However, while environments like these can lead to levels of extreme misconduct and corruption, Moskos maintains that the institution of policing is not corrupt overall.

Good leadership, committed to transparency and accountability, could make the difference, Moskos suggested.

"Leadership sets the tone through a certain amount of transparency, the discipline process they utilize, and their own behavior," he said.

In a 2008 study on how leadership affects officers taking gratuities, an analysis of three separate police forces in The Netherlands identified the key factors that made one police agency less susceptible to corruption than the other two:

- Management provided a clear definition of the acceptable norms;
- Encouraged openness and discussion from line officers, including a requirement to report any gratuities received;
- The agency was led by an involved police commissioner who played a central role in the establishment of those norms.

Could U.S. police forces achieve the same level of internal trust and transparency?

The EPIC Approach

"You really have to change the way you approach this issue," said Jonathan Aronie, the federal monitor overseeing the New Orleans Police Department (NOPD). "Make sure that officers are never in the position of having to choose between doing the right thing and not because, in some environments, those decisions are hard to make."

Responsible for reviewing, assessing, and reporting publicly on their compliance with a 2013 Consent Decree, Aronie assisted the NOPD in creating Ethical Policing Is Courageous (EPIC), a peer intervention program tool that teaches officers how to more effectively intervene in another officer's conduct to prevent mistakes, misconduct, and promote health and wellness.

On the whole, officers don't want their colleagues to get in trouble and they don't want their colleagues to violate the law, so if you have a better, safer and more effective way to tell your partner, 'sit this one out and I'll take it from here,' most people will use that tool," Aronie said.

Such approaches represent a major departure from the harsh discipline that most officers fear if they step out of line, and could help call early attention to those who are experiencing the kind of stress or behavioral issues that boil over into over-aggressive policing on the street.

"If there are incidents you see that look like misconduct, there is a high likelihood there was a health and wellness issue somewhere in the past," said Aronie.

Aronie, who serves as an instructor at the FBI National Academy's professional development course for U.S. and international law enforcement leaders, said the majority of the officers in his classes regularly acknowledge that their departments are continually underperforming when it comes to monitoring the health and wellness of their officers.

He maintains that EPIC can be a solution to this problem.

"Every time I teach EPIC, I tell the officers real life stories about misconduct and mistakes," said Aronie.

"I give them three stories and I ask which one of these could have been prevented with EPIC? They always answer 'all three of them.'"

Daily exposure to violence and trauma on the beat can also result in hyper-aggressive behavior, according to a 2015 study for the Walden University College of Social and Behavioral Sciences.

Another study, a 2018 report by the federal Office of Community Oriented Policing Services found that behavioral dysfunctions associated with Post-Traumatic Stress Disorder (PTSD) can, if untreated lead to mental impairment and substance abuse.

"On the whole, police departments do a poor job on officer health and wellness," said Aronie.

"They underserve their officers, which means that they underserve their communities. EPIC is one of the few programs that hits these problems from all angles and, even in a dysfunctional department, it's still going to save careers and lives. It's still better than not having it."

Since its creation, aspects of EPIC have been developed and incorporated into training by departments in North Carolina and Clemson University. Law enforcement agencies in Dallas, Burlington, Vt., and Ithaca, N.Y., have since followed suit.

These are steps in the right direction, but even the most promising policies can sometimes fail.

The Risks of Intervention

The Minneapolis Police Department, which has been on the firing line since the Floyd death, implemented an intervention policy in 2016, stating that it is an officer's duty to intervene and stop or attempt to stop another sworn employee when force is being inappropriately applied or is no longer required.

The rule did not prevent three Minneapolis officers from standing by during the killing of Floyd by their colleague Derek Chauvin.

Chauvin was their training officer. He had at least 16 other misconduct complaints over two decades.

Officers inclined to intervene cross the line at their risk.

In 2014, when former Buffalo Police Officer Carol Horne intervened to stop a fellow officer from punching and choking an arrested man, the officer punched her in the face. She was later fired and charged with obstruction.

According to Joseph Moseley, a 32-year veteran of the Chicago Police Department, retribution for whistleblowing will continue unless there are reforms to the how internal affairs investigations are conducted.

"If you look at the Internal Affairs divisions in Chicago, and you start looking at the names, in most cases their officers are either second generation or they're married to different people in the force," said Moseley

"How am I going to go to internal affairs to report misconduct when half the guys in internal affairs have family members on the job?"

Is Misconduct Contagious?

Another troubling lesson from research: misconduct can be contagious.

According to a study published in the journal Nature Human Behavior, for every 10 percent increase in the proportion of a police officer's peers with a history of misconduct (for instance, adding one allegedly misbehaving member to a group of 10), that officer's chances of engaging in misdeeds in the next three months rose by nearly 8 percent.

This is exemplified by cities like Chicago and Minneapolis. Both police departments have displayed a pension for violence, corruption and general misconduct that has spread like a disease from officer to officer with little to no successful efforts in place for containment or prevention.

To tackle this issue, Moseley insists that departments should take a page out of the Federal Bureau of Investigation (FBI) playbook.

"The FBI operates off a thing called 'candor'; it's basically their ethics clause," said Moseley.

"It starts from the ground level, the day you walk in, and it's chargeable."

A review of the FBI's disciplinary system by the Department of Justice states that, under FBI policy, employees must report all allegations of misconduct to appropriate FBI officials, who are, in turn, required to report them to the DOJ Office of the Inspector General.

"If they enacted those same parameters to local law enforcement, a lot of this misconduct would probably wipe itself out," Mosley argued.

Lack of Legal Protection for Whistleblowers

A good first step, according to experts contacted by TCR, is enshrining protection for police whistleblowers in state statutes.

"The lack of legal protection for officers making reports about the conduct of fellow officers is a problem," said Ann Hodges, Professor of Law Emirata at the University of Richmond.

In a 2018 study, Hodges found that while most states now have whistleblower protection laws in place for public employees who choose to speak out against their employers, a 2006 Supreme Court decision went in the other direction for law enforcement.

The ruling in *Garcetti v. Ceballos* effectively removed Constitutional protection from retaliation for officers who report unlawful conduct through their chain of command, she said.

"Police officers have a duty to report and take action with respect to unlawful conduct. That's their job, but *Garcetti* says that if you're speaking out as a part of your job duties you don't have First Amendment protection and you can be retaliated against or fired."

The theory behind this decision is that it prevents bad employees from being able to claim retaliation when and if they are terminated from their employment. However, Hodges points out that this reasoning creates a limitation on remedies for employees who are legitimately retaliated against, and that the whistleblower protections or civil service statutes that states may have in place saying, for example, that an employer cannot terminate someone without cause often have limitations of their own.

"With respect to the First Amendment protections and whistleblower laws, those protections are not there for the employees who are speaking pursuant to their job duties," said Hodges.

"And it isn't always termination you need protection from. Maybe you're transferred to the night shift, maybe you're moved to a more dangerous place to do police work. Even if you have protection and have to be fired for cause they can make your life pretty miserable in other sorts of ways."

After *Garcetti,* potential whistleblowers are left exposed.

In order to make it easier for officers to protect themselves while also exposing misconduct, Hodges recommends a return to the "Pickering balancing test," a once-common court practice that resulted from the 1968 Supreme Court decision in *Pickering v. Board of Education and* served to buttress whistleblowing cases for three decades before being overturned by Garcetti.

"*Pickering* says that if they're speaking out on a matter of public concern, which clearly this would be if someone is reporting serious misconduct by a police officer, then the court will balance the employee's and the public's interests in the speech vs. the employers interests in taking some sort of action," Hodges said.

John Kostyack, executive director of the National Whistleblower Center (NWC), a U.S. nonprofit providing legal assistance to whistleblowers and advocating for stronger whistleblower protection laws, believes that changes like this are necessary if police departments are to be brought to task for retaliating against the men and women who are just doing their jobs properly.

"When retaliations happen it needs to be more than just getting your job back," said Kostyack.

"There has to be serious compensation that sends a strong message."

However, Kostyack believes that, in general, police departments are not at the forefront of creating effective whistleblower programs, and that in order to effect change, states and their courts must be pushed to create very clearly stated anti-retaliation laws and principles that force departments into compliance and offer sever sanctions for those that violate them.

"State legislatures could fix *Garcetti v. Ceballos* in a heartbeat," said Kostyack.

He sees Idaho as a perfect example. In 2015, Idaho State Police Detective David Eller filed a lawsuit against his department after management retaliated against him for testifying against a fellow officer who faced a vehicular manslaughter charge after a fatal crash in 2011.

With the help of the NWC, Eller was able to eventually win his case, earning a $1.29 million settlement for lost wages, legal fees and damages including emotional distress.

"That's an example of how you could build a program that sends a strong enough message that retaliation is taken seriously by the state and will be penalized," said Kostyack.

However, change is slow, and the culture of silence and retribution in policing is commonplace in departments around the country.

Complicating the problem, there are roughly 18,000 state, county and local law enforcement agencies in the United States today. With no national standards, two departments in two neighboring towns can have completely different rules and policies.

Changing one does not mean the others have to follow suit.

As a result, misconduct in police departments continues while small changes and major failures occur seemingly at random and are dealt with in the same fashion. Meanwhile, good police are forced to decide between speaking up and losing everything they hold dear in the process.

Even, at times, their lives.

"There's a legitimate fear of real retribution," said Moskos. "A bullet through your window kind of retribution."

But it's in the interests of officers as well as the communities they serve to end a culture that rewards silence and concealment, said Spalding.

"Most officers go to work to serve and protect and will die for you," she said. "We have to find a way for these officers to safely speak out about serious civil rights violations and crimes.

"These kinds of crimes need to be reported."

| "The short answer to 'are
| whistleblowers safe from retaliation'
| is 'not necessarily.'"

Police Whistleblower Retaliation Is Real

Christopher Brown

In this viewpoint, Christopher E. Brown examines why police whistleblowers have even less protection against retaliation than members of the general public. Even though retaliation is technically not allowed in police departments, the fact that there are no direct penalties for retaliation encourages this kind of behavior. A Supreme Court case called Garcetti v. Ceballos *ruled against police whistleblowers, making the act of reporting misconduct even more unsafe than it previously was. Brown describes a number of ways in which police whistleblowers have been harassed for doing what they thought was right. Christopher E. Brown, Esq. is the principal attorney of the Brown Firm PLLC.*

As you read, consider the following questions:

1. Why did the *Garcetti v Ceballos* decision rule against protecting police whistleblowers?
2. What are some specific ways in which whistleblowers have been retaliated against?

3. What is Brown's advice to police whistleblowers concerned about potential retaliation?

E very police officer has a duty to protect and uphold the peace and safety of the public, and this oath can lead law enforcement into dangerous and even deadly situations. The high stress of the job, personal biases and beliefs, situational challenges, and other issues can lead to an officer making the wrong decision about handling a particular incident.

When a law enforcement officer makes a choice that violates an individual's civil rights, such as through excessive force, nonconsensual sexual contact or discrimination, among many other possibilities, that officer may be reported through a process called whistleblowing.

What Is Considered Whistleblowing?

Whistleblowing is the act of revealing unacceptable behavior by "blowing the whistle" and alerting authorities or the relevant organizations about its occurrence. A whistleblower may come from within the police department itself if another officer raises the alarm about the behavior of his or her colleagues.

A whistleblower case is not necessarily limited to a single individual; someone can choose to alert authorities about department-wide issues if multiple officers are participants. For example, if an entire police department is complicit in establishing a team-wide agreement to pull over people of a certain race, a whistleblower may raise the alert about the entire department.

Naturally, most human beings (police officers included) dislike being confronted about their behavior, giving many potential whistleblowers pause due to concerns about retaliation. Many people do not know whether they have any rights or protections as soon as they blow the whistle on police misconduct.

Are Whistleblowers Protected from Retaliation?

The short answer to "are whistleblowers safe from retaliation" is "not necessarily." Especially in cases in which another officer is the whistleblower, protection may vary from individual to individual. If a member of the public makes a report about police misconduct, officers are not permitted to retaliate against this report; however, there is no direct penalty for retaliation in this case. The retaliation is itself considered misconduct, but it is not illegal in the strictest sense.

If a police officer comes out as a whistleblower in their own department, they see even less protection than a member of the public. Public employees who speak out against their company of employment may enjoy whistleblower protection laws; however, a Supreme Court decision in 2006 removed such protection for officers who make these reports.

The relevant case, *Garcetti v Ceballos*, made the decision not to offer First Amendment protection against retaliation given the consideration that bad employees may abuse the ability to claim retaliation if terminated from their jobs. Thus, depending upon the context, a whistleblower may not be able to benefit from any legal protection and may be retaliated against.

What Does Whistleblower Retaliation Look Like?

Whistleblower retaliation can come in many forms, but perhaps the most famous case is of Frank Serpico, a detective of the New York Police Department who became a whistleblower to out widespread corruption in the department in the 60s.

Other whistleblowers who have faced retaliation have seen behavior such as dead rats being placed on the windshield of their car, being pulled over frequently for no apparent reason, being transferred to different departments and even being terminated from their employment. In some cases, whistleblowers have found that the most permanent and least stressful solution to retaliation is to move out of state.

However, although not all whistleblowers are protected (unless you are a federal employee), reporting unacceptable behavior is not guaranteed to result in any negative consequences and is still a critical part of keeping the police accountable for their behavior and preventing their negative actions from impacting the public.

If you are concerned about the potential repercussions of making a whistleblower claim, you must reach out for legal guidance to ensure that you are protected as much as possible.

> *"Many people will claim that the vast majority of cops are 'good' and that we shouldn't let public opinion be tainted by 'a few bad apples'. But if this is the case, why aren't the police doing more to police themselves?"*

Video Evidence Helps Break Through the Code of Silence

Rosie Parry and Jean-Pierre Benoît

In this viewpoint, Rosie Parry and Jean-Pierre Benoît consider the logic of the George Floyd murder case from a number of angles. They go over the facts of the incident, and, near their conclusion, apply Baynesian reasoning to the case, which is a method for updating the probability of a hypothesis as new information becomes available. First, they ask whether a reasonable officer would kill an unarmed subject who committed Floyd's crime. Next, they consider the mitigating factors in the situation. Finally, they turn to the evidence of the video to make a logical determination that the mitigating factors do not overturn the reality that Chauvin acted unreasonably and violated George Floyd's rights. Rosie Parry is a writer living in London. Jean-Pierre Benoît is a professor of economics and Chair of the Economics Faculty at the London Business School.

"What 'the Blue Wall of Silence' Means for Police Reform," by Rosie Parry and Jean-Pierre Benoît, London Business School, October 14, 2021. © Think at London Business School. Reprinted by permission.

As you read, consider the following questions:

1. What crime had George Floyd committed when he was arrested?
2. What was Derek Chauvin's previous police record?
3. Why is the video of the George Floyd incident so important?

Floyd was a father, truck driver and mentor. He died last year, when one of the four police officers involved in his arrest, Derek Chauvin, knelt on his neck for over nine minutes. Floyd was unarmed and accused only of attempting to use a counterfeit twenty-dollar bill in a local convenience store. As he lay dying, other officers involved stopped passers-by from intervening, but were unable to stop video footage of the event from being uploaded to social media, where it was swiftly shared across the globe.

In the weeks that followed, unrest in Minneapolis sparked action around the country. Tens of thousands of Americans marched against unchecked police brutality and Floyd's cry of "I can't breathe" became an unofficial slogan for the Black Lives Matter movement.

Along with the protests came discussions about the future of policing. Is it possible to reform a police force where a man like Chauvin thrived? Or should the police be defunded entirely, with money channelled towards social work and community care instead? Suddenly, these once radical ideas were becoming part of mainstream American discourse.

One of the major hurdles to reform is how police respond—or don't—to accusations of corruption. Often, allegations are met with silence from other officers, who will almost never testify against each other in court.

Professor Jean-Pierre Benoît addressed the issues surrounding the wall in his lecture "The blue wall of silence, the killing of George Floyd, and Bayesian reasoning." Here's what it means for the debate:

Just a Few Bad Apples?

Derek Chauvin was convicted of second-degree unintentional murder, third-degree murder, and second-degree manslaughter. We might look at this and feel that at least justice has been served, but unfortunately Chauvin is the exception. Police officers are rarely convicted of serious crimes, or even internally disciplined. Chauvin himself had eighteen official complaints of misconduct on his record, and was still a serving officer, still allowed to carry a gun.

"A pervasive code of silence" influences both honest and corrupt officers and leaves even the "good" cops reluctant to report brutality.

What does a case like Chauvin's tell us about policing in modern America? Is it evidence of broader corruption, or just a "bad cop" gone rogue? Many people will claim that the vast majority of cops are "good" and that we shouldn't let public opinion be tainted by "a few bad apples." But if this is the case, why aren't the police doing more to police themselves?

The blue wall of silence refers to police officers' well-documented refusal to speak out against their own. From procedural errors, to serious crimes, officers will almost never report a colleague's misconduct. In the court room, officers rarely testify against each other, often going so far as to perjure themselves by feigning ignorance. Police unions too, are notorious for defending officers, seemingly regardless of their actions.

The wall gets its name from the blue uniforms worn by American officers, but this is not a uniquely American phenomenon. Nor is it a new one; The City of New York Commission to Investigate Allegations of Police Corruption and the Anti-Corruption Procedures of the Police Department, concluded in 1994 that "a pervasive code of silence" influences both honest and corrupt officers and leaves even the "good" cops reluctant to report brutality.

Why Does It Exist?

For many officers, the police force is a brotherhood. A family. Only other officers understand the reality of the job, the brutality of the streets and the danger they put themselves in every day. Essentially, only cops understand cops. This belief has led to an insular culture, where protecting one of their own is second nature. Those who do speak out are often ostracized, which makes other officers less likely to come forward. Some former officers have even claimed they were harassed or threatened after testifying against a colleague.

The Wall is Damaging to Police and Public Trust

These silent tactics are often so entrenched that they have become counterproductive. The wall is so infamous, it has come to be expected. Often, investigators will factor this in and essentially ignore positive police testimonies or disregard union statements. The public too has largely become inured to these statements. Clearly, the more unilaterally officers are defended, the less weight those defences carry.

Of course, there is also a moral cost for many officers. People join the police force to catch criminals, don't they? It can be extremely distressing for officers to realise that sometimes those criminals are within their own ranks.

What Chauvin's Defence Tells Us About Police Brutality

We can pick a case like Chauvin's apart very logically and use that logic to tell us something about police brutality more broadly. Clearly, when an innocent person dies at the hands of an officer, something has gone very wrong. But could it have somehow been an understandable mistake?

Often, in cases like these officers will use the "split second" defence, claiming they had just moments to act and were afraid for their lives. Or they might claim the victim was holding something—a phone, a pack of cigarettes, even a toy—that looked like a weapon.

In reality, these defences have a damning. If deaths like Floyd's can be explained away as having been somehow "reasonable," then where does this leave us? Are we to conclude that a "good" cop acting reasonably is just as likely to kill an innocent person as a "bad" cop?

Video Evidence Makes All the Difference

Chauvin's team used all these defences and more. But in this case, everything came back to the video. We can clearly see Chauvin's knee on Floyd's neck. Floyd is handcuffed, distressed, calling out for his mother and unable to breathe. Even after he stops moving, Chauvin keeps his knee there for another two or three minutes. It is indefensible.

Chauvin knows he's being filmed, but does he look worried? Does he modify his behaviour for the camera? No. The reality is that Chauvin doesn't worry he's being filmed because he does not believe he will be punished.

There Will Be No Reform While the Wall Exists

Protestors didn't take to the streets because they believed Chauvin was one bad apple. They marched against systematic injustice and the culture of silence that allows officers like Chauvin to exist. Chauvin behaved as he did because nothing in his training or work environment suggested to him that he would face consequences for brutalising an innocent black man.

In Minnesota, the blue wall of silence did wilt during Chauvin's trial. The police chief acknowledged that Chauvin acted wrongly. This must continue if public trust is ever to be restored. Otherwise, there is no difference between "good" and "bad" cops, and reform will remain impossible.

This wilting of the blue wall came tragically late. If most people had eighteen complaints against them, they would be severely disciplined, if not fired. Why is this not the case for police officers? Why isn't the force throwing these abusive officers, before someone dies?

How Can We Use Bayesian Reasoning to Assess Chauvin's Case?

Bayesian inference is a method for updating the probability of a hypothesis as new information becomes available. If we want to assess whether an officer who killed an unarmed person was acting criminally when they killed someone, we can interrogate two areas: our understanding of the specific events that led to the death and our existing beliefs about the American police force.

Firstly, we need to ask what is the probability that a police officer would kill an unarmed person when acting reasonably? How much less likely is this than a police officer killing an unarmed person when acting criminally? To the extent that a reasonable officer is less likely to kill an unarmed person, the facts themselves tend to point to criminal behaviour.

However, we must also look beyond the event itself. Let's say we take the view that most police are "good"—the defense is often counting on this being the starting point of the jurors (and the public at large). Arguments like the "split-second" defence, or claims the victim was on drugs, can cloud the issue, leading jurors (and other observers) to lean heavily on their pre-existing beliefs and decide the officer was more likely to be reasonable than criminal—or at least not criminal beyond a reasonable doubt.

But in the case of the killing of Floyd, there is the video. No matter how favourable one's view of the police might be, there is no denying Chauvin's brutality. The video is crystal clear, and the first half of the Bayesian odds is too strong to be overturned by the second. Chauvin is clearly guilty.

> *"I personally believe this code of silence is a positive virtue in police work. Police officers, unlike any other group of workers, must believe in and trust their fellow officers with, not only their lives, but with their futures."*

The Code of Silence Is a Necessity in Police Work

Larry Casey

Former police sergeant Larry Casey admits in this viewpoint that there is a police code of silence, arguing that in the unique world of policing, it is necessary to allow the police to do their jobs effectively. He argues that the majority of workers in other professions share a code of silence as well. In police work, officers must trust their colleague with their lives and futures. Casey believes that those outside of the profession simply do not understand how individual officers make judgments on how to handle situations. Casey says that he is not arguing that gross misconduct shouldn't be penalized; however, he believes that when officers make honest mistakes, they should be given a pass. Larry Casey is a retired police sergeant in the Chicago Police Department, and a professor of criminal justice at Wilbur Wright College.

As you read, consider the following questions:

1. Why does Casey question his students about petty offenses?
2. For what reason does Casey compare police officers to lawyers, surgeons, and politicians?
3. Why does Casey say that the code of silence is mostly an honorable one?

Is there a code of silence on the Chicago Police Department? Absolutely yes. Police officers tend to protect their own in minor situations: so do doctors, mechanics, bankers, donut makers, attorneys and just about every profession known to mankind.

As I teach at a local college, I had the opportunity to ask my students, whose ages range between 18 and 60 years old, what type of jobs they do. I asked the mechanic if he ever works on his personal automobile while in the shop and on company time. I asked the girl in the donut shop if she ever took donuts home without paying for them. I asked the clerk if he ever took office supplies home without paying for them. This went on for 30 minutes. All those questioned responded that they took things without paying for them and/or witnessed other workers taking things without paying for them. From my little experiment I concluded that the vast majority of people share a code of silence in their workplace.

I personally believe this code of silence is a positive virtue in police work. Police officers, unlike any other group of workers, must believe in and trust their fellow officers with, not only their lives, but with their futures. The only other profession on earth to equal that level of trust is the military.

Our dilemma is that there is no absolute response to any police scenario that can be taken as gospel. As such, officers with diverse personalities are inherently going to respond differently in different situations. Sometimes these responses are going to be physical and often seen as excessive. Some responses in certain situations are excessive, but if used under other circumstances, would be appropriate.

Did I Earn My Pension?

Faultfinders don't take this perspective into consideration. Nor do they allow the officer to use his empirical knowledge and personal discretion in determining the correct course of action. Simply said, there is no manual or book of instructions that every officer can adhere to, so when an officer does overstep his boundaries, he should be reined in and corrected, not fired and sued.

A proactive police officer cannot go a year on the streets without inadvertently or accidentally violating another person's civil rights. A slap or a kick is going to take place following a threat to the officer's daughter from some druggy or after a high speed chase that puts innocent lives in jeopardy. These reactions are human and reactive, also provoked by the criminal. This is where I have the biggest problem. Politicians, news media and police bosses believe that officers should be robots without emotions. They think in terms of theory, not reasonableness or the real world.

Let's look at other groups: The murder suspect you just arrested always says you have the wrong guy, the burglar or stick up guy always denies guilt, the corner dealer adamantly states those aren't his drugs. These are all nefarious individuals so we understand why they lie. So let's explore the famous and highly respected professions.

The surgeon leaves the dead patient on the operating table after a failed routine procedure. How often does he admit to the family that he inadvertently slipped and accidentally killed his patient? How about the defense attorney that repeatedly and knowingly lies to the judge about his client's innocence. Let's look at the accountant compiling his tax returns. How about the dentist describing his patient's need for expensive dental work to the insurance company? And the ultimate prize, how about the politician seeking re-election and the intentional false promises made?

Who's Got Your Back?

By no means am I trying to make any case for officers to violate the law. If a police officer steals money or drugs, he should be held fully accountable. What I am saying is if a police officer makes an honest mistake, treat him with fairness and reasonableness.

Also, often misinterpreted as lying, is when an officer on the scene of a traumatic incident gives a differing version of what occurred. When a police officer is confronted by a life changing scenario like a shooting, he goes through a phenomenon termed tunnel vision. This is when the officer's line of vision reduces to a fraction of normal and their brain focuses on the immediate threat while ignoring other surrounding issues.

Secondary officers are often accused of filing false reports because their views don't always accurately mimic what occurred. This phenomenon has been repeatedly explained by medical professionals and repeatedly ignored by police oversight professionals.

Police officers are human and sometimes overreact. This, by itself should not be grounds for any overzealous discipline. Police officers should be held to a higher standard but we are still human beings with a normal range of emotions. Officers that violate the civic trust by stealing from people and committing other deliberate criminal acts should be held accountable. Police officers cannot be judged by typical means, their jobs are much too complicated.

Is there a code of silence? Yes, in all professions and walks of life. Interestingly, the code of silence in police work is mostly an honorable one compared to all other professions. Should we ignore the code of silence in police work? No, but we should attempt to understand it further and while respecting the officer's constitutional rights, we should determine the real right or wrong and never judge officers based on the normal man's moral base. There is nothing normal about police work.

What are your views?

Periodical and Internet Sources Bibliography

The following articles have been selected to supplement the diverse views presented in this chapter.

Gina Barton, Daphne Duret and Brett Murphy, ""Behind the Blue Wall of Silence," *USA Today*, December. 9, 2021. https://www.usatoday.com/in-depth/news/investigations/2021/12/09/blue-wall-police-misconduct-whistleblower-retaliation/8836387002/.

City University of Seattle, "Law Enforcement and Mental Health: Breaking the Code of Silence," the *Seattle Times*, February 28, 2020. https://www.seattletimes.com/sponsored/law-enforcement-and-mental-health-breaking-the-code-of-silence/.

Mark C. Curran, Jr. "'Codes of Silence' Threaten the Public, No Matter Who Adheres to Them," *National Review*, September 2, 2020. https://www.nationalreview.com/2020/09/police-codes-of-silence-threaten-public/.

Timothy Egan, "The Blue Wall of Silence Is Starting to Crack," the *New York Times*, April 16, 2021. https://www.nytimes.com/2021/04/16/opinion/police-brutality-chauvin-minnesota-chicago-virginia-blue-wall.html.

Kevin Gosztola, "Facing Felony Trial, Joliet Police Whistleblower Who Exposed Black Man's Death Retires," Scheerpost, July 26, 2022. https://scheerpost.com/2022/07/26/facing-felony-trial-joliet-police-whistleblower-who-exposed-black-mans-death-retires/.

Joe Grimm, "The Blue Wall of Silence and the Police Killing of George Floyd," Spartan News Room, April 16, 2021. https://news.jrn.msu.edu/culturalcompetence/2021/04/16/the-blue-wall-of-silence-and-the-police-killing-of-george-floyd/.

Philip Hayden, "Why an Ex-FBI Agent Decided to Break Through the Blue Wall of Silence," *USA Today*, January 31, 2019. https://www.usatoday.com/story/opinion/policing/2019/01/31/blue-wall-of-silence-policing-the-usa-cops-community/2604929002/.

Michael Hirsh, "Serpico on Police Racism: 'We Have This Virus Among Us," *Foreign Policy*, June 11, 2020. https://foreignpolicy.com/2020/06/11/george-floyd-protests-serpico-police-racism-good-cop/.

Laura Iheanachor, "Breaking Down the Blue Wall: What Congress Can Do," CREW, February 24, 2022. https://www.citizensforethics.org/news/analysis/breaking-down-the-blue-wall-what-congress-can-do/.

Matt Katz, "How to Protect Whistleblowers Calling Out Police Misconduct," WNYC Studios, May 6, 2022. https://www.wnycstudios.org/podcasts/otm/segments/how-protect-whistleblower-rights-on-the-media.

Sanja Kutnjak Ivković, Jon Maskály, Ahmet Kule and Maria Maki Haberfeld, "The Pressing Need to Study the Code of Silence," *Police Code of Silence in Times of Change*, April 5, 2022. https://link.springer.com/chapter/10.1007/978-3-030-96844-1_1.

Isidoro Rodriguez, "The Plight of the Police Whistleblower," the Crime Report, June 18, 2020. https://thecrimereport.org/2020/06/18/the-plight-of-the-police-whistleblower/.

Frank Serpico and Tom Devine, "To Change the Culture of Silence, Protect Police Whistleblowers," the *Hill*, July 8, 2020. https://thehill.com/opinion/criminal-justice/505994-to-change-the-culture-of-silence-protect-police-whistleblowers/.

Sarah Shulte, "Chicago Police Code of Silence Not Broken; Whistleblowers Must Be Protected to Get Change, Experts Say," ABC 7, April 21, 2021, https://abc7chicago.com/derek-chauvin-george-floyd-video-police-code-of-silence/10535574/.

Brent Sprecher, "Real Cops Who Stood Up to Corruption in Their Departments (and What Happened to Them)," Ranker, September 23, 2021. https://www.ranker.com/list/police-department-whistleblowers/brent-sprecher.

CHAPTER 4

Are Government Whistleblowers Heroes or Traitors?

Chapter Preface

Alexander Vindman was a lieutenant colonel in the U.S. Army and director for European Affairs for the United States National Security Council (NSC). Born in Ukraine, Vindman had emigrated with his family to the United States at the age of three. He later joined the U.S. Army, fought in Iraq, and was awarded a Purple Heart after being wounded by an explosive device.

Vindman's life changed in July of 2019 when, as part of his regular duties, he listened in on a phone call between then-President Donald Trump and the recently elected President of Ukraine, Volodymyr Zelenskyy. In the buildup to the Russian invasion of Ukraine in February 2022, Congress had authorized $400 million for Ukrainian defense. But President Trump had held up this money, hoping that Zelenskyy could help Trump in his bid for reelection. Hunter Biden, the son of Trump's successor, had worked for a company in Ukraine called Burisma, which had paid him a substantial amount. Trump was hoping Zelenskyy's government could investigate Hunter Biden and provide the Trump campaign with material to use against his 2020 presidential challenger.

As Vindman listened to the phone call between Trump and Zelenskyy, all the while taking notes, he heard the president say to his Ukrainian counterpart, "I would like you to do us a favor...."[1] Trump was asking for a *quid quo pro*: he would release the defense funds for Ukraine that he was illegally holding up in exchange for what the Russians called "*kompromat*": compromising information collected for use in blackmailing, discrediting, or manipulating someone, typically for political purposes.

A seasoned veteran of international affairs, Alexander Vindman knew immediately that what he was hearing was problematic. His twin brother, Yvgeny, known as Eugene, was an ethics officer for the National Security Council. In his memoir, *Here, Right Matters*, Alexander Vindman said that he knew that if the gist of the phone call became public, President Trump would be impeached.

The brothers took their concerns to John Eisenberg, who was the senior attorney for the National Security Council. Days later, they were told not to talk about it to anyone. That fall, Alexander Vindman testified before Congress, laying out the illegal *quid pro quo* to which he was a first-hand witness. As a result, President Trump faced the first of his two impeachment hearings.

Vindman knew that he would face retaliation for testifying at the impeachment hearing. Addressing his father's concerns for his welfare, he told his father, Congress, and the world, "Dad, my sitting here today … is proof that you made the right decision 40 years ago to leave the Soviet Union and come here to the United States." He went on: "Do not worry, I will be fine for telling the truth."[2] Vindman faced down a barrage of right-wing attacks from Trump allies, Republicans in Congress, and media outlets such as Fox News. Some accused him of being a Ukrainian spy.

Trump was acquitted of the charges when the Senate, as everyone knew beforehand, was unable to muster the 60 votes necessary to remove him from office.

The acquittal occurred on a Wednesday. Two days later, human resources informed Vindman that his services were no longer needed. He was walked out of the White House. "…the most powerful man in the world—buoyed by the silent, the pliable and the complicit—has decided to exact revenge," said Vindman's lawyer, David Pressman.[3]

But Vindman was still a lieutenant colonel in the U.S. Army, having served with distinction, and at the time was expecting a promotion, along with hundreds of other officers. The White House was determined that Vindman would not get his promotion. They threatened to hold up the promotions of all of the other officers just to retaliate against Vindman. So Alexander Vindman did what he believed to be best and retired from the military.

Despite being drummed out of his job and his commission, Alexander Vindman still believes he did the right thing and, even in hindsight, would not have changed his course of action. In the aftermath of his ordeal, Vindman has told the media that he is indeed "fine," and is pursuing opportunities outside of government. But it is clear that being a government whistleblower is fraught with dangers, and only the stout of heart need apply.

Notes

1. "Read Trump's Phone Conversation with Volodymr Zelensky," CNN, September 26, 2019. https://www.cnn.com/2019/09/25/politics/donald-trump-ukraine-transcript-call/index.html.
2. Frida Ghitis, "Vindman's Poignant Message to His Dad," CNN, November 19, 2019. https://www.cnn.com/2019/11/19/opinions/vindman-message-to-his-father-ghitis/index.html.
3. Dan Mangan, "Trump's 'Revenge'—Impeachment Witness Alexander Vindman Escorted from White House, Lawyer Says," CNBC, February 7, 2020. https://www.cnbc.com/2020/02/07/trump-impeachment-witness-vindman-escorted-out-of-white-house.html.

> "In the contemporary era, the U.S.
> has executed only two spies, Ethel
> and Julius Rosenberg, who were
> American citizens accused of
> transferring atomic secrets to the
> Soviet Union. That sentence outraged
> millions of Americans and continues
> to stir controversy."

Differentiating Whistleblowers from Spies

Marc Favreau

In this viewpoint written during the Trump presidency, Marc Favreau traces the history of espionage during the Cold War to distinguish between spies and whistleblowers. Then-President Trump had declared that a government whistleblower was engaging in espionage against the U.S. and even suggested that the penalty for such actions could be execution. But Favreau points out that the whistleblower was acting in a completely different manner from a spy and therefore could not be considered guilty of espionage. Calling a whistleblower a spy is a way of casting them in a negative light, but their goals are very different. Marc Favreau is the author of Spies: The Secret Showdown Between America and Russia.

As you read, consider the following questions:

"Whistleblower or Spy? What the History of Cold War Espionage Can Teach US," by Marc Favreau, History News Network, November 3, 2019. Reprinted by permission.

1. What are some of the roles that spies took on during the Cold War?
2. What was the greatest danger for a spy, according to the viewpoint?
3. According to Favreau, how is a whistleblower different from a spy?

President Donald Trump has called the source for the author of the whistleblower complaint "close to a spy," and alluded to the harsh treatment supposedly meted out to spies in an earlier era. Many observers were appropriately wary of the president's definition, as whistleblowers have a unique history in our system— and legal protections—that go back to the nation's founding.

In fact, Trump is not totally wrong in embracing a somewhat more expansive definition of espionage than our common media stereotypes might suggest. The modern history of espionage, to the extent that it can be known, provides something of a guide in assessing Trump's accusation, as well as his proposed punishment.

Since the dawn of the Cold War and the rapid expansion of the CIA's covert operations program (alongside the work of other agencies charged with surveillance and espionage work, including especially the National Security Agency) spies have taken on a vast range of assignments and assumed many different roles. Codebreakers, high-altitude pilots, tunnel-diggers, sound engineers, counter-surveillance and counterespionage specialists— all of these have played crucial roles in America's modern spy wars.

Of course, covert operatives, of the sort we typically associate with espionage, have been the unsung heroes of America's efforts to glean vital information about its real or potential adversaries. These women and men have little in common with James Bond or Jason Bourne; instead, they are masters of the psychology of persuasion, of assumed identities, and above all of transferring information from source to headquarters. In their essential book *Spycraft*, Robert Wallace and H. Keith Melton write that "for a spy the greatest danger usually is not stealing a secret, but passing it to his handler … Without the means to transfer information securely between agent and handler, espionage could not exist."

Indeed, when we think about the role of the spy, the transit of information—from an often unstable, even dangerous source (whether a U-2 spy plane, the Berlin Tunnel, or a mole operating deep inside the Kremlin) to government officials who can interpret and deploy this information for strategic purposes—seems to be the defining feature.

Trump's claim that the whistleblower committed espionage puts us in uncharted territory. The interesting twist here is that it's not the purported spy who is serving as a conduit of information in conjunction with a foreign regime—that conduit, of course, *is the president himself.* Instead, the whistleblower/spy conducted her or his operation entirely within the scope of the executive branch of the U.S. government and followed established protocols, which in this instance involved sending a letter to the Inspector General of the Intelligence Community (ICIG). Whatever we might think of the whistleblower's motives, he or she has sought identification *as a whistleblower*—precisely the kind of exposure a spy would never seek.

Trump's suggested punishment for the whistleblower/"spy"—execution—raised justifiable concern from many political commentators. In the contemporary era, the U.S. has executed only two spies, Ethel and Julius Rosenberg, who were American citizens accused of transferring atomic secrets to the Soviet Union. That sentence outraged millions of Americans and continues to stir controversy. The Soviets, in contrast, executed many of their own citizens accused of collaboration with foreign espionage services, typically deep inside Lefortovo Prison, the KGB dungeon in Moscow. Lest we consider that as a model, we should recall that the Soviet Union's treatment of prisoners and dissidents received so much international condemnation, it led to the creation of Helsinki Watch in 1978, a key moment in the modern human rights movement.

As the Cold War progressed, both sides adopted a very different practice for dealing with captured spies on enemy soil. An unmasked covert operative was termed *persona non grata* and promptly ejected ("PNG'd") from the host country—generally ruining a promising undercover career and depriving a spy service of precious human talent. Many spies on both sides of the Iron Curtain met this fate, but were fortunately able to return home to productive senior roles inside their respective spy services. Given this history, therefore, is it possible imagine that our whistleblower/spy might be sent home to his or her original agency, and in fact get a promotion? Clearly, the spying analogy has led us to something of a dead end.

The world of spies is one of deceptions and defections; the whistleblower, in contrast, stepped into a sharply-defined role in sending the complaint letter to the Inspector General. It's not difficult to understand why the president and his defenders wish to paint the whistleblower in an unflattering light, but they will find no support for their cause in the history of espionage.

> *"In order to punish elected officials for engaging in narrow opportunism, voters must possess information about their wrongdoing. The issue is that acquiring the requisite information is costly."*

Whistleblowing and the Importance of Going Public

Christopher J. Coyne

According to Christopher J. Coyne, whistleblowers are indispensable for checking government opportunism. Additionally, he argues, in some cases it is best for said whistleblowers to make their accusations public, rather than go through government channels. This circumvention may be necessary because there are so many ways in which a whistleblower's information can be used, abused, ignored, or misinterpreted. Whistleblowers may also face retaliation for reporting their information internally, so, in some cases, they can be most effective by publicizing their knowledge through the media. A concern with allowing whistleblowers to go public is that they may engage in self-interested opportunism. Laws that encourage truthful public whistleblowing are a necessity. Christopher J. Coyne is a professor of economics at George Mason University and the Associate Director of the F. A. Hayek Program for Advanced Study in Philosophy, Politics, and Economics at the Mercatus Center.

As you read, consider the following questions:

1. According to Coyne, what is a principal-agent problem?
2. How does widespread voter ignorance occur?
3. What are three factors that limit the effectiveness of
   congressional oversight?

W histleblowers play a crucial role in democratic societies. Recognizing this function is important for fully appreciating Patrick Eddington's call for reforms to protect whistleblowers as well as the limitations of relying on channels internal to government institutions for whistleblowers to report wrongdoing. My purpose is twofold. First, I discuss why whistleblowers are important in democracies for checking political opportunism. Second, I consider why being an effective whistleblower might involve going public and circumventing formal government channels.

Democratic politics is characterized by numerous principal-agent problems. A principal-agent problem exists whenever one person (the "agent") is able to make a decision on behalf of another person ("the principal"). Absent incentives to align the interests of the two parties, there is the potential for agent opportunism whereby the agent pursues their own interests instead of those of the principal they are hired to represent. Citizens are principals who "hire" elected officials to serve as their agents by representing their interests in political matters. Elected officials, in turn, are also principals who hire bureaucrats as their agents to provide goods and services to their constituents. Mechanisms, such as citizen voting and congressional oversight, are intended to solve these principal-agent problems by aligning incentives. But a large literature in public choice has highlighted various frictions that limit their effectiveness.[1]

In order to punish elected officials for engaging in narrow opportunism, voters must possess information about their wrongdoing. The issue is that acquiring the requisite information is costly. As policy becomes more complex it becomes increasingly difficult for voters to obtain the necessary information and to discern the specific role played by their representatives. This becomes even more difficult when the required information is kept secret by those in government. These factors are especially important in matters of national security and foreign policy, which are often highly nuanced and where members of the U.S. government are all too comfortable classifying information to restrict access.[2]

Even where information is available, voters are often subject to "rational ignorance" due to the cost of obtaining information relative to the benefits. Simply put, the cost of acquiring information is positive while the benefits are often minuscule given the limited influence of a single vote on electoral outcomes. The result is widespread voter ignorance which limits the effectiveness of the voting booth as a check on political opportunism.[3] Another issue is that each voter only receives a single vote which limits their ability to express the intensity of their dissatisfaction with elected officials. There is also the issue of the timing gap between elections, which further limits the ability of voters to punish or reward elected officials. The long delays between elections further limit the effectiveness of the voting booth as a check on political opportunism.

What about congressional oversight of bureaus? There are three issues which weaken the effectiveness of this check. The first is the aforementioned over classification of information, which limits the access to certain members of Congress. Second, members of Congress often rely on the bureaus they oversee to supply information regarding their activities. The issue is that members of the bureau can control the flow of information, both in terms of content and the timing of its release, which is being used to monitor their actions. Third, members of congressional oversight committees may have the incentive to ignore wrongdoing by the bureaus they monitor. When discussing congressional oversight of the National Security Agency (NSA), James Bamford noted that "the intelligence committees are more dedicated to protecting the agencies from budget cuts than safeguarding the public from their transgressions."[4] Together, these factors limit the ability of congressional oversight to solve the principal-agent problem.

Within this context the role of whistleblowing is clear. Whistleblowers serve as a means of resolving the principal-agent problem in democratic politics.[5] They do so by avoiding many of the issues facing individual voters and members of Congress. Whistleblowers have access to local and context-specific information regarding abuses of political power. Because they are embedded in the organization and have direct experience, whistleblowers have nuanced knowledge about the operations of government that outsiders—both voters and congressional members—cannot have. This direct knowledge also allows whistleblowers to circumvent the constraints created by secrecy and classification. For the same reason, whistleblowers do not suffer from issues of information control and manipulation by bureaus since they are the source of information.

Given the role of whistleblowers, how are they to report on wrongdoing? There are two methods. The first relies on formal, internal channels to report abuse. This is the focus of Patrick Eddington's lead essay. He accurately describes the limitations, and in many instances the complete lack, of protections for whistleblowers. I agree with his call for reform. However, I would extend his discussion by emphasizing the importance of a second avenue for whistleblowing reporting—going public. This second channel involves whistleblowers reporting information to the public either directly or through a third party, such as the media. I believe this option is necessary even if Eddington's proposed reforms were implemented. The reason is that there will still be frictions that may limit the effectiveness of formal, internal channels for reporting wrongdoing.

The normal operations of government can move extremely slowly due to bureaucratic inertia. Consider the case of Richard Levernier, who worked for the U.S. Department of Energy to identify weaknesses in plans to protect its nuclear plants from terrorist attacks. After identifying numerous weaknesses and threats through formal channels, Levernier was stripped of his security clearance and reassigned to a clerical position. It took four years for the United States Office of Special Counsel (OSC), the independent federal agency tasked with protecting whistleblowers, to investigate and rule that the Department of Energy's retaliation was unlawful. Perhaps a better-designed review process might have led to a faster resolution, but this case illustrates how the sluggishness of bureaucratic processes in general can delay the protection of whistleblowers even when they follow established formal rules.

In addition to inefficiencies with formal rules, there are informal norms which often discourage internal whistleblowing. As Daniel Ellsberg notes, "[t]he mystique of secrecy in the universe of national security, even beyond the formal apparatus of classification and clearances, is a compelling deterrent to whistleblowing and thus to effective resistance to gravely wrongful or dangerous policies. In this realm, telling secrets appears unpatriotic, even traitorous."[6] Such an insular culture limits the effectiveness of even well-designed formal rules for internal reporting by whistleblowers.

The major concern with allowing whistleblowers to go public is that they too may engage in narrowly self-interested opportunism. This is one justification used to limit public whistleblowing through severe penalties. Given the important role of whistleblowers, these penalties create a problem by discouraging both narrowly opportunistic and truthful whistleblowers from revealing information. What is needed are mechanisms which create a separation between the two categories of whistleblowers.

One set of rules is offered by Patrick Rahill who proposes a multi-factor test for courts when considering whether an act of whistleblowing was legal.[7] This includes a consideration of intent on the part of the whistleblower, the type of information leaked, the recipient of the leaked information, and whether the leak was done in the public interest. While one could envision variations of the specific rules, the central idea is the importance of incentivizing truthful whistleblowers to go public, while discouraging those motivated by narrow self-interest. Rules which encourage truthful public whistleblowing are a complement to Eddington's proposed reforms to formal, internal channels for whistleblowing. Together, these reforms would maximize the chances of whistleblowers serving as effective checks on political abuse and opportunism.

Notes

[1] For an overview of public choice see, Dennis C. Mueller, Dennis C. 2003. Public Choice III. Cambridge, MA: Cambridge University Press; Charles K. Rowley and Friedrich Schneider. 2004. The Encyclopedia of Public Choice. 2 vols. New York: Springer; Michael Reksulak, Laura Razzolini, and William F. Shughart II. 2014. The Elgar Companion to Public Choice, 2nd Edition. Northampton, MA: Edward Elgar Publishing, Inc.

[2] On the over classification of national security information, see Steven Aftergood. 2009. "Reducing Government Secrecy: Finding What Works," Yale Law & Policy Review 27(2): 399-416; Elizabeth Goitein and David M. Shapiro. 2011. Reducing Overclassification Through Accountability. New York, NY: The Brennan Center for Justice at New York University School of Law.

[3] See the Cato Unbound discussion on "Is Smaller Government Smarter Government?" October 2013.

[4] James Bamford. 2013. "Five Myths about the National Security Agency," The Washington Post, June 21.

[5] For a more detailed treatment of this point, see Christopher J. Coyne, Nathan Goodman, and Abigail R. Hall. 2019. "Sounding the Alarm: The Political Economy of Whistleblowing in the US Security State," Peace Economics, Peace Science, and Public Policy, 25(1): 1-11.

[6] Daniel Ellsberg. 2010. "Secrecy and National Security Whistleblowing," Social Research 77(3): 773-804.

[7] Patrick M. Rahill. 2014. "Top Secret—The Defense of National Security Whistleblowers:
Introducing a Multi-Factor Balancing Test," Cleveland State Law Review 63: 237-267.

> *"The media glorifies those who risk everything to expose corruption and illegal activity and rightly so; these lionized individuals deserve every ounce of praise they receive. But their happy outcomes are not typical—for every success story, there are a hundred stories of professional martyrdom."*

Exposing Government Corruption Can Be Professional Martyrdom

Steven Aftergood

In this viewpoint, Steven Aftergood considers the case of government whistleblower Jesselyn Radack. When John Walker Lindh—the "America Taliban"—was arrested in 2001, he was interrogated without an attorney, a breach of law that caused Radack to blow the whistle. Her career with the Justice Department was subsequently destroyed because of her truthfulness and desire to do the right thing. The media often glorifies people like Radak, but in her case there was simply silence. Radack has since joined the Government Accountability Project, where she has used her own experience to help promote whistleblower rights. Steven Aftergood directed the Federation of American Scientists (FAS) Project on Government Secrecy from 1991–2021. The project is aimed at reducing the

"'Traitor,' A Whistleblower's Tale", by Steven Aftergood, Federation of American Scientists (FAS), April 16, 2012. Reprinted by permission.

scope of national security secrecy and to promote public access to government information.

As you read, consider the following questions:

1. What were some of the ways in which the government retaliated against Jesselyn Radack?
2. How does Radack characterize the Bush and Obama administrations' attitude toward government whistleblowers?
3. According to the viewpoint, why is "whistleblower" a loaded term?

Jesselyn Radack's memoir *Traitor: The Whistleblower and the American Taliban* presents the moving story of a young attorney's unexpected encounter with official misconduct, and the excruciating ordeal that ensued when she decided to challenge it.

In 2001, Ms. Radack was a Justice Department attorney and specialist in legal ethics. In response to an official inquiry, she advised that the newly captured John Walker Lindh, the so-called "American Taliban," should not be interrogated without an attorney present—which he then was anyway. When department officials publicly denied having received any such legal advice, and even destroyed evidence to the contrary, she exposed the deception.

Ms. Radack was not looking for a fight, but only to do the right thing. For her trouble, she was forced out of her Justice Department position, put under criminal investigation, fired from her subsequent job, reported to the state bar, and put on the "no fly" list.

Traitor is the story of a young professional whose career is derailed because her ethical compass will not let her be silent in the face of official dishonesty. It is also the story of a political system that is seemingly incapable of tolerating honorable dissenting views within the government workforce.

While a handful of "whistleblowers" become figures of popular acclaim, or heroes of movies such as *The Insider* or *Erin Brockovich*, they are the exception rather the rule, Ms. Radack writes.

"The media glorifies those who risk everything to expose corruption and illegal activity and rightly so; these lionized individuals deserve every ounce of praise they receive. But their happy outcomes are not typical—for every success story, there are a hundred stories of professional martyrdom. Mine is one of them."

Ms. Radack eventually found a measure of redemption as an attorney with the Government Accountability Project where she has turned her own experience to advantage in promoting whistleblower rights. She was among the most stalwart and effective defenders of Thomas Drake, the former NSA official and whistleblower whose dubious prosecution under the Espionage Act ended with the dismissal of all felony charges against him.

The Bush administration (in which she worked) was hostile to whistleblowers, according to Ms. Radack, but the Obama administration is even worse.

"The Bush administration harassed whistleblowers unmercifully," she writes. "But it took the Obama administration to actually prosecute them."

I don't think it is true, however, that the prosecution of Drake "was a test case for the Justice Department to try a novel legal theory… that the Espionage Act could be used to prosecute leakers" (p. 159).

Far from being novel, the use of Espionage Act to prosecute unauthorized disclosures of classified information predates the Drake case by decades. At least since the conviction of Samuel L. Morison in the 1980s for providing classified intelligence imagery to Jane's Defence Weekly—and the Supreme Court's refusal to review the case—this application of the Espionage Act has been seemingly well established.

And there is some ambiguity about who qualifies for the appellation "whistleblower." It is a loaded term both because it presumes the pure intention of the individual challenger, and because it takes for granted the corruption of his target. These need to be demonstrated, not simply asserted. It cannot be the case that a strong sense of personal conviction, untethered from legal or ethical constraints, is enough to entitle anyone to be called a whistleblower. If that were so, then Jonathan Pollard and other disreputable figures could claim the title.

THE ESPIONAGE ACT IS MISUSED TO PUNISH GOVERNMENT WHISTLEBLOWERS

As we wrote on the 100th anniversary of the Act's passage, the Espionage Act was designed to prosecute spies who disclosed military secrets to foreign nations, not sources who disclose newsworthy information to the press. Unfortunately, the Espionage Act has been misused throughout its existence, from silencing left-wing speech during the Red Scare days of its origin to the indictments of whistleblowers such as Daniel Ellsberg, Chelsea Manning, and Edward Snowden.

As the ACLU's Jay Stanley sets out, the Espionage Act is particularly ill-suited and perhaps unconstitutional when used against government whistleblowers who share information with the press. Among other defects, the Espionage Act provides no public interest defense to a leaker, and contains no requirement that the government prove the information as properly and appropriately classified in the first place. Moreover, because a great number of leaks are either encouraged or at least tolerated by the U.S. government when they serve the government's purpose, the Espionage Act provides a mechanism for the selective punishment of government critics rather than furthering the general interests of preserving classified information.

The Espionage Act is currently the basis for the charges against Reality Leigh Winner, the former federal intelligence contractor who is accused of leaking a National Security Agency memo containing information regarding Russian hacking attempts against a U.S. voting software supplier.

The Espionage Act is as poor a fit for prosecuting Winner, as it was for going after other journalists' sources.

"Misused Espionage Act Targets Government Whistleblowers," by David Greene, Electronic Frontier Foundation, August 1, 2017.

Ms. Radack states twice that the Obama administration has prosecuted leakers "who more often than not were whistleblowers" (p. 69, 92). This suggests that she thinks at least some of the six leak defendants to have been prosecuted by the administration may not have been whistleblowers. But if so, she does not specify which ones they were, or why she came to that conclusion.

I would say that "whistleblowers" are not a separate category of people in any essential sense. Anyone can act with integrity under some circumstances. The whistleblowers that we honor are people who act with integrity under extreme duress and sometimes at great cost. Radack's memoir is an eloquent account of one such case.

> *"Asked if it is appropriate to prosecute whistleblowers using the Espionage Act, Sanders said, 'Of course not.'"*

Bernie Sanders and Alexandria Ocasio-Cortez Reject Use of the Espionage Act to Arrest Whistleblowers

Ryan Grim

In this viewpoint, written during Senator Bernie Sanders' run for the Democratic presidential nomination in 2019, Ryan Grim writes about how Sanders, if elected, claimed he would have eliminated the use of the Espionage Act to prosecute government whistleblowers. The Espionage Act was revived under the Obama and Trump administrations to prosecute certain government whistleblowers. In using it, these administrations essentially consider leakers to be spies, and getting a fair trial is nearly impossible. Representative Alexandria Ocasio-Cortez has stated that she believes the prosecution of whistleblowers such as Reality Winner is anti-democratic. Interviewed at the same time as Sanders, Ocasio-Cortez said she believes that journalists and whistleblowers hold elected officials accountable. Ryan Grim is the Intercept's *DC Bureau Chief. He was previously the Washington bureau chief for HuffPost, where he led a team that won the Pulitzer Prize.*

"Bernie Sanders Pledges to End Practice of Prosecuting Whistleblowers Under the Espionage Act," by Ryan Grim, The Intercept, October 23, 2019. Reprinted by permission.

As you read, consider the following questions:

1. Why do Sanders and Ocasio-Cortez believe that the Espionage Act is being used incorrectly?
2. How did former President Trump handle government whistleblowers?
3. What did Reality Winner do that caused officials to invoke the Espionage Act?

As president, Bernie Sanders would end the practice of using the controversial Espionage Act to prosecute government whistleblowers, the Vermont senator told The Intercept in an interview on Saturday ahead of a major rally in New York.

The century-old law had largely gone out of fashion until it was deployed heavily by the Obama administration, which prosecuted eight people accused of leaking to the media under the Espionage Act, more than all previous presidents combined. President Donald Trump is on pace to break Barack Obama's record if he gets a second term: He has prosecuted eight such whistleblowers, five of them using the Espionage Act, according to the Press Freedom Tracker.

Asked if it is appropriate to prosecute whistleblowers using the Espionage Act, Sanders said, "Of course not."

The Espionage Act, which was passed in 1917 to suppress opposition to World War I and now considers leakers to effectively be spies, makes a fair trial impossible, as relevant evidence is classified and kept from the defense, and the bar for conviction is low. The law also comes with stiffer criminal penalties and longer sentences than more obvious charges that might be leveled, such as mishandling classified intelligence.

During the interview, The Intercept noted that Trump has referred to White House officials, who provided information to the whistleblower who went through legally sanctioned channels and alerted Congress of Trump's Ukraine activities, as "spies." Democrats widely condemned Trump for the comparison, though those same Democrats have not generally objected to the Justice

Department's use of the Espionage Act to prosecute whistleblowers who leak to journalists, suggesting that the media is being treated tantamount to a foreign adversary. "Whistleblowers have a very important role to play in the political process," Sanders said in response. "And I am very supportive of the courage of that whistleblower, whoever he or she may be."

Asked if he would give a second look at the record-setting length of the sentence doled out to National Security Agency contractor Reality Winner, Sanders demurred, saying that he was supportive of whistleblowers but unfamiliar with her case.* Rep. Alexandria Ocasio-Cortez, D-N.Y., who joined Sanders during the interview, agreed. "I don't want to speak out of turn when it comes to Reality Winner, but I just think that the prosecution of whistleblowers is frankly against our democracy. We rely on whistleblowers, we rely on journalists, in order for us to hold our systems accountable." Winner was sentenced to 63 months for leaking a top-secret NSA document related to Russian interference in the 2016 U.S. election to a news organization that was widely reported to be The Intercept. She is currently being silenced in prison.

Update: October 22, 2019

During the back and forth about Winner, a protester repeatedly shouted lewd remarks toward Ocasio-Cortez, and the clip has been edited out of the full video. A transcript of the exchange is below:

> Grim: Last one. President Trump referred to the whistleblower in the White House as a spy, and a lot of Democrats jumped on him for that. But his administration and the last one have both used the Espionage Act to prosecute leakers. Do you think the Espionage Act should be used to prosecute leakers?

> Sanders: The law is very clear: Whistleblowers have a very important role to play in the political process, and I am very supportive of the courage of that whistleblower, whoever he or she may be.

> Grim: Last one. Reality Winner is serving the longest sentence...

Sanders: I'm sorry?

Grim: Reality Winner is serving the longest sentence of any whistleblower. She's the one who — she's the only reason that we know about Russia's attempt to interfere in our actual election process. Do you think that her sentence deserves a look …

Sanders: I'm honestly unfamiliar with that, but in general, I mean, when somebody has the courage to be a whistleblower, I think that that person should be supported.

Grim to Ocasio-Cortez: Have you followed that case?

Ocasio-Cortez: Yeah. You know, I think, and again, I don't want to speak out of turn when it comes to Reality Winner, but I do think that the prosecution of whistleblowers is frankly against our democracy. We rely on whistleblowers, we rely on journalists in order for us to hold our systems accountable.

> "Snowden boasts more than 5m
> Twitter followers and regularly
> speaks about privacy issues
> via satellite interviews. His
> revelations and thoughts about
> privacy and security are never far
> from the headlines, stoking fear
> and incredulity."

Edward Snowden Deserves a Fair Trial

Caroline Byrne

In this viewpoint, Caroline Byrne writes about Edward Snowden and how he leaked thousands of classified documents in 2013. She quotes Richard Ledgett, former National Security Agency (NSA) official, who claims that Snowden's leaks put people in danger. But Snowden himself claims that there is no proof the documents contain harmful information. Even some government officials believe that Snowden helped open the debate over privacy in the U.S. Snowden, who fled to Russia, was charged under the Espionage Act, but, according to Byrne, this hasn't deterred other government leakers such as Daniel Hale, Chelsea Manning, and Reality Winner. U.S. officials state that it is clear Snowden broke the law, and he remains a fugitive, asking only for a fair trial in the U.S. Caroline Byrne writes for Spyscape.

As you read, consider the following questions:

1. Why is the American public unclear about what exactly Edward Snowden did?
2. How did former Director of National Intelligence James Clapper change his thinking about Snowden?
3. What spy "tradecraft" did Snowden employ to expose government documents?

When Edward Snowden leaked thousands of NSA intelligence documents in 2013 he triggered an international debate: Is Snowden a hero or a traitor?

Russia's decision to grant Snowden Russian citizenship in September 2022 has rekindled the war of words.

Richard Ledgett, former deputy director of the NSA, has called Snowden's leaks "inappropriate." "He put people's lives at risk in the long run," Ledgett said. "I know there's been a lot of talk by Edward Snowden and journalists who say the things disclosed did not put national security or people at risk. That is categorically not true. They actually do."

A 2016 report by the House Permanent Select Committee on Intelligence concluded that "the public narrative cultivated by Snowden and his allies is rife with falsehoods, exaggerations, and crucial omissions" and that "the vast majority of the documents he stole have nothing to do with programs impacting individual privacy interests—they pertain instead to military, defense, and intelligence programs of great interest to America's adversaries."

Snowden's Tweeted response to the Committee's findings? "After three years of investigation and millions of dollars, they can present no evidence of harmful intent, foreign influence, or harm. Wow."

The former CIA employee has become an unlikely poster boy for privacy campaigners, however. His defenders included journalist Glenn Greenwald, *The Guardian* reporter who first published documents provided by Snowden that detail the NSA

PRISM program to monitor the phone calls and emails of U.S. citizens. "Every time there's a whistleblower—somebody who exposes government wrongdoing—the tactic of the government is to try and demonize them as a traitor," Greenwald told ABC News.

In 2020, Snowden said that he and his wife were applying for Russian citizenship to ensure they would not be separated from their Russian-born son in the midst of the pandemic lockdowns and closed borders.

Whistleblower or Criminal?

James R. Clapper, former Director of National Intelligence (DNI), initially denounced Snowden's whistleblowing as "reckless" in June 2013, saying the leaks had done "huge, grave damage" to U.S. intelligence capabilities.

Months later, however, Clapper accepted that Snowden may have done a public service by starting a healthy debate about the balance between privacy and security.

"As loath as I am to give any credit for what's happened here, which was egregious, I think it's clear that some of the conversations that this has generated, some of the debate, actually probably needed to happen," Clapper said, according to *The Los Angeles Times*. "It's unfortunate they didn't happen some time ago, but if there's a good side to this, that's it."

Within two years, the U.S. Patriot Act was amended to prevent the NSA from bulk collecting phone records in a victory for privacy advocates.

In 2020, the NSA surveillance program Snowden exposed was ruled illegal by the U.S. Court of Appeals for the Ninth Circuit. Judges found that the warrantless telephone dragnet that hoovered up millions of Americans' telephone records without their knowledge violated the Foreign Intelligence Surveillance Act and may have been unconstitutional.

"I never imagined that I would live to see our courts condemn the NSA's activities as unlawful," Snowden tweeted after the 2020 ruling.

The Appeals Court judgment didn't clear the way for Snowden to return to the U.S., however. He remains a fugitive from U.S. justice in Russia, where he fled after leaking NSA intelligence.

Spy Tradecraft

The Snowden story is steeped in modern tradecraft. He used complex operational security, psyops, signals intelligence, social engineering, and encryption during his time with the CIA and later as an NSA contractor, then applied his skills to effectively extract and leak classified documents from them. From pre-assigned codewords and secure messaging apps to Rubik's cubes and "security blankets," there was no shortage of fascinating tradecraft at play.

Greenwald initially ignored Snowden's step-by-step guide on how to secure his email communications. Frustrated, Snowden then contacted filmmaker Laura Poitras, who applied more acceptable encryption. Eventually, Snowden delivered documents to both and arranged to meet them in a Hong Kong Hotel.

Snowden instructed Greenwald and Poitras to meet him in a specific district (Kowloon), at a specific place (a shopping mall with large crowds). He told them to wait until they saw a man carrying a Rubik's cube, then ask him about a restaurant in the mall.

Snowden allowed Greenwald and Poitras to question him for a week in his hotel room. The first article, titled *NSA collecting phone records of millions of Verizon customers*, was published on June 6, 2013, by Greenwald in *The Guardian*. It immediately became worldwide news.

"I don't want to live in a world where every expression of creativity or love or friendship is recorded," Snowden had told the journalists. "That's not something I'm willing to support, it's not something I'm willing to build, and it's not something I'm willing to live under. So I think anyone who opposes that sort of world has an obligation to act in the way they can."

On the Run

In June 2013, Snowden checked out of his Hong Kong hotel and fled. His plan was to fly to Moscow, then on to Cuba, and finally Ecuador, where he would seek asylum. The U.S. government annulled his passport on the first leg of this journey, however, trapping him in the Moscow airport.

Russia offered Snowden asylum, which the U.S. condemned. According to a May 2013 criminal complaint, the American government charged Snowden under the Espionage Act of 1917 with theft of government property, unauthorized communication of national defense information, and willful communication of classified communications intelligence information to an unauthorized person.

The charges against Snowden haven't deterred more U.S. government whistleblowers from coming forward, however. Daniel Hale, who leaked classified information about drone warfare intelligence to the press, was charged under the Act as was Chelsea Manning, a former U.S. Army intelligence analyst who provided WikiLeaks with hundreds of thousands of classified documents.

Reality Winner, who leaked classified NSA information about Russia's interference in the 2016 presidential election, was sentenced to more than five years in 2018 after passing top-secret documents to a news website. She was released early in 2021.

Much like Snowden, there is ongoing debate as to whether Hale, Manning, and Winner are heroes, traitors, or possibly a bit of both.

Whistleblower or Criminal?

U.S. federal law broadly protects whistle-blowers with one exception, employees who are privy to the nation's secrets, said Professor Richard E. Moberly of the University of Nebraska College of Law.

"The definition of a whistle-blower depends on the context," he said. "Outside of national security we tend to think very broadly.

[Whistle-blowers expose] not only illegal activity, but abuses of power, fraud, financial misconduct, and even unethical choices."

But employees entrusted with state secrets "should be more limited in how and what to disclose," he said.

Under U.S. law, intelligence employees have their own system to report activity they believe violates the law or is unethical. Employees are instructed to report wrongdoing to Congress, or up their chain of command, to the Director of National Intelligence, or to their agency's inspector general, Moberly said.

Snowden, who has lived in Moscow since 2013, is now a household name worldwide. He has won numerous awards including the Thomas S. Szasz Award for Outstanding Contributions to the Cause of Civil Liberties in 2020. He was also nominated for the 2016 Nobel Peace Prize.

Snowden boasts more than 5m Twitter followers and regularly speaks about privacy issues via satellite interviews. His revelations and thoughts about privacy and security are never far from the headlines, stoking fear and incredulity.

"What I took away from reading the Snowden documents was that if the NSA wants into your computer, it's in. Period," cryptographer Bruce Schneier said in Gordon Corera's book *Intercept*.

Eric Holder, former U.S. Attorney General of the United States, credits Snowden for starting a public debate on privacy but has previously said that he'd still punish him: "He broke the law. He caused harm to our national security and I think that he has to be held accountable for his actions."

Edward Snowden has not sought a presidential pardon, although others have done so on his behalf. He plans to remain abroad until his one condition is met: "My condition for return is simply a fair trial."

> "Across more than two centuries,
> the United States has repeatedly
> confronted the challenge of relying on
> state secrecy when the public interest
> requires it, while resisting the misuse
> of secrecy to advance the private
> interests of those in power."

Edward Snowden and Chelsea Manning Are Flawed, and Perhaps Traitorous, Whistleblowers

Hudson Institute

In this review of the book Secrets and Leaks: The Dilemma of State Secrecy *by Rahul Sagar, the authors consider the history of government whistleblowing in America. They begin by discussing two competing interests in statecraft: the need for secrecy, weighed against the public's right to know and to hold their leaders accountable. Because the judiciary and Congress are limited in their ability to check executive power, whistleblowers may serve a useful role. Sagar proposes a five-part test to determine whether a whistleblower should leak information. Contemporary whistleblowers such as Snowden and Manning do not fare well on Sagar's test; they therefore seem more like traitors than patriots. The Hudson Institute is a research organization that challenges conventional thinking and helps manage strategic transitions through interdisciplinary studies in defense, international relations, economics, energy, technology, culture, and law.*

"Whistleblowers and Traitors: A Review of 'Secrets and Leaks' by Rahul Sagar," Hudson Institute, May 6, 2014. Reprinted by permission.

As you read, consider the following questions:

1. How are Congress and the judiciary limited in their ability to check executive (presidential) power?
2. What are the five parts of Sagar's whistleblower test?
3. Why do Snowden and Manning not fare well on Sagar's whistleblower test?

All government requires secrecy, but self-government requires transparency. The core governmental activities needed to promote national security—diplomacy, military preparations and actions, and intelligence in all its forms—are never conducted according to a rule of full disclosure. But governments that derive their just powers from the consent of the governed jeopardize their own legitimacy if they withhold or distort information the governed need to assess the governance to which they are consenting. Governmental secrecy not only impedes the formation of sound public judgment, but can facilitate abuses of power. Arthur Schlesinger, Jr., once noted that although secrecy is sometimes necessary, it more frequently served "to protect the executive branch from accountability for its incompetence and its venality, its follies, errors and crimes."

Across more than two centuries, the United States has repeatedly confronted the challenge of relying on state secrecy when the public interest requires it, while resisting the misuse of secrecy to advance the private interests of those in power. Today, more than ever, this is a fraught issue in American life. Thanks to Edward Snowden, Chelsea Manning, and a host of others, the American public is learning about highly secret matters, like the techniques of domestic surveillance, with which it is vitally concerned. Yet we are also being warned by responsible officials that exposing those secrets is damaging our ability to fight terrorism, thwart nuclear proliferation, compete with aspiring powers like Russia and China, and protect our other interests around the globe. The result is a fierce national debate about defining and enforcing the limits of secrecy. Rahul Sagar's *Secrets and Leaks: The Dilemma of State Secrecy*, which emerged out of a Harvard doctoral dissertation, could not be more timely.

Sagar, who now teaches politics at Princeton, begins at the beginning, with the American Founding. He persuasively refutes the view, shared by Schlesinger and others, that the framers of the Constitution favored nearly unlimited transparency. Exploring 18th-century republican thought, he finds a wealth of evidence demonstrating that the leading thinkers of the day took it for granted that statecraft requires, in the words of Scottish Enlightenment philosopher Francis Hutcheson, "secret and speedy execution" if it is to succeed. The practical men who devised our Constitution—in secret proceedings behind closed doors—designed institutions in which secrecy had a place even as they understood it could generate a host of evils.

Having examined our intellectual and legal traditions, Sagar takes up the central question: which institutions in the framers' system have the power to ensure that secrecy is employed only for proper ends? The Catch-22 is that identifying abuses of secrecy requires access to the very material being kept secret. That is the fundamental "dilemma" noted in Sagar's subtitle, and the framers were almost entirely silent about how to resolve it.

Two centuries of historical experience have provided work-arounds, but none is altogether satisfactory. The third branch of government—our judicial system—is one potentially powerful check on executive secrecy. The courts, after all, possess the authority to review executive branch compliance with the laws mandating transparency. Thus, the Freedom of Information Act requires disclosure of government documents on request, but also exempts nine categories of information, creating plenty of ambiguity and room for litigation. When the government has been challenged, courts have been extraordinarily deferential to the executive branch, ruling that it alone has the responsibility and the competence to determine what kinds of disclosures might cause harm.

A fascinating case in point discussed by Sagar is the 1980 Freedom of Information Act suit brought by activist Morton Halperin, who asked the CIA to disclose the identity of some private attorneys it retained, as well as the fees it paid them. The CIA argued that neither the names nor sums could be disclosed, lest it "give leads to information about covert activities that constitute intelligence methods." Explaining how such information could lead to that result, the agency maintained that "[i]f a large bill is incurred in a covert operation, a trained intelligence analyst could reason from the size of the legal bill to the size and nature of the operation." This seems implausible, and on its face even an abuse of the government's power to withhold information from the public. Federal judge Malcolm Wilkey ruled for the CIA, however, explaining that "a court, lacking expertise in the substantive matters at hand, must give substantial weight to agency statements." Such judicial deference—rooted in the fact that the separation of powers entails a division of labor and competencies—has limited the judiciary's ability to patrol the boundaries of executive branch secrecy.

Congress could serve as a check on it, too, but Sagar shows how its own institutional handicaps compromise legislators' ability to do so. Though vested with considerable power regarding national security and foreign affairs, Congress has a very limited capacity to monitor, let alone discipline, secret operations of the sprawling executive branch. The president and his subordinates, in turn, are justifiably apprehensive about sharing highly sensitive matters with a body composed of so many members. As a result, they regularly invoke executive privilege to avoid an accidental, or intentional, security breach.

Sagar entertains various reform proposals to expand the scope of congressional oversight, like sharply curtailing the deployment of executive privilege or creating a core group in Congress empowered to oversee everything the executive branch does. He rejects the former on the grounds that anything less than absolute secrecy would sometimes imperil national security and Americans' lives, as in 1979's "Canadian caper" in Iran, the subject of the movie *Argo*. And he rejects the latter approach for not really addressing the fundamental dilemma at all. Permitting only a small number of elected representatives to know all executive branch secrets will not allay fears about the abuse of secrecy. Rather, the members of this core group will themselves become the objects of suspicion insofar as "their own conduct as overseers is shielded from public view." In the end, Sagar concludes that given the executive branch's "stranglehold over the flow of national security information, there is little reason to believe that lawmakers will be able to *take the lead* in uncovering policies and actions that the president has decided to conceal" (emphasis in the original).

This brings Sagar to the most interesting and original section of his fascinating book: the press and its interaction with "whistleblowers." He examines whether leaks can be a useful "regulatory mechanism" for constraining untoward executive secrecy. The dilemma is that while leaks can serve as an "effective and credible" means of policing the executive, their unlawful nature undermines their legitimacy. A system where leaks are not condemned but condoned would have serious consequences and be fundamentally anti-democratic. The parties involved in leaks—government bureaucrats who illicitly disclose confidential information, and journalists who disseminate it—are self-appointed, private arbiters. Allowing leakers and journalists to determine what constitutes an illegitimate government secret, argues Sagar, "violates the democratic ideal that such decisions should be made by persons or institutions that have been directly or indirectly endorsed by citizens." When, instead, the decisions about which secrets are kept and which revealed are made by government officials exceeding their authority, by the journalists they leak to, and by the publishers who run the journalists' revelations, the leaks "constitute a form of usurpation."

Sagar shows that whistleblowers often disclose wrongdoing within government, but their particular form of law-breaking is not always civil disobedience properly understood. He specifies five conditions that whistleblowers must meet if they are to be lauded, not condemned, for violating the web of regulations and laws in which they are situated. First, their revelations must disclose genuine wrongdoing, which is more often contestable than clear. In particular, a disagreement over policy is not the same as an accusation of illegality, though all too often self-appointed whistleblowers collapse the distinction. Second, the evidence a whistleblower adduces to demonstrate his claim of governmental misconduct must be "clear and convincing," not "fragmentary." Third, an unauthorized disclosure "should not impose an undue or disproportionate burden on national security." Putting out "the truth at any cost" is illegitimate in circumstances where it does more harm than good, which can be the case when the country is under threat or at war. Fourth, the whistleblower should "utilize the least drastic means of disclosure" by exhausting all avenues for complaint within the federal government before going outside it to the press. Finally, anonymity is a perversion of democratic norms, making it "difficult for the public to discern whose interests the disclosure is serving, and to take appropriate steps to counter the possibility of manipulation."

This five-part test can be criticized, but Sagar methodically considers and cogently answers various objections. In actual practice, the complexities of governance mean that his test may not equip us in every case to make crisp judgments about the ethics of disclosure. But it provides a useful starting place for thinking about whistleblowing. In particular, his framework condemns the behavior we see on display today from Snowden and Manning, both of whom fall far short of meeting Sagar's qualifications for justifiable leaks. Snowden meets only one of the five criteria: he disclosed his own identity. But he chose to do even that from Hong Kong and Russia, locations beyond the reach of American law. This was civil disobedience without the consequences, which is not civil disobedience at all. (Agreeing to subject oneself to the possibility of prosecution and punishment should have been Sagar's sixth condition. Choosing a life in exile as a fugitive from justice has nothing in common with civil disobedience.) Considering the immense damage Snowden has done to our national security, and the way he did it, Snowden is less whistleblower than traitor. Some of the journalists who were awarded Pulitzer prizes for obtaining and disseminating Snowden's revelations have assiduously—and to my mind, disingenuously—sidestepped this distinction, calling Snowden simply a journalistic "source." Others among them—adherents of an extreme left-wing brand of libertarianism—have preferred to laud him as a hero.

Manning also does not fare particularly well on Sagar's grid. If she had stopped with the video she provided to WikiLeaks of two Apache helicopters firing their cannons at targets in Iraq, she would have had at least a prima facie case to be considered a whistleblower, even though the Pentagon's subsequent legal reviews found no evidence of illegal conduct by American forces in this incident. But Manning did not stop there. Her anonymous and indiscriminate leaking of a vast trove of sensitive documents is precisely what turned her into the malefactor now serving a long military prison sentence.

The Snowden and Manning cases are relatively easy to assess, but other leaks—some of them far less damaging to our security and also quite informative to the public—are today the daily substance of our national news outlets. At the same time, the extent of governmental secrecy has become an urgent subject of discussion and debate. Although Sagar's *Secrets and Leaks* bears too many traces of a doctoral dissertation to attract a broad audience, it is a thoroughly researched, thoughtfully considered work that clarifies an unsolvable dilemma at the heart of democratic governance.

Periodical and Internet Sources Bibliography

The following articles have been selected to supplement the diverse views presented in this chapter.

Michael E. Bednarczuk, "Whistleblowers Serve a Vital Function. Governments Should Treat Them Better," *Governing*, April 29, 2022. https://www.governing.com/now/whistleblowers-serve-a-vital-function-governments-should-treat-them-better.

Louis Clark and Brian McLaren, "Potential Whistleblowers Deserve More Support. Their Moral Choices Protect Our Democracy," *USA Today*, February 13, 2021. https://www.usatoday.com/story/opinion/2021/02/13/whistleblowers-protect-democracy-we-must-protect-them-column/4406728001/.

Michael E. DeVine, "Intelligence Community Whistleblower Provisions," *Congressional Research Service*, June 15, 2022. https://sgp.fas.org/crs/intel/R45345.pdf.

Maya Efrati, "Opinion: We Need to Change the Way We Talk About Whistleblowers," Whistleblower Network News, March 15, 2019. https://whistleblowersblog.org/opinion/we-need-to-change-the-way-we-talk-about-whistleblowers/.

Brit McCandless Farmer, "Reality Winner and the Debate over the Espionage Act,"*CBS News*, December 5, 2021. https://www.cbsnews.com/news/reality-winner-espionage-act-60-minutes-2021-12-05/.

Dana Gold, "Viewpoint: Whistleblowers are Democracy's Last Defense," Government Executive, November 18, 2020. https://www.govexec.com/management/2020/11/viewpoint-whistleblowers-are-democracys-last-defense/170147/.

Liz Hempowicz, "The State of Whistleblower Protections and Ideas for Reform," POGO. January 28, 2020. https://www.pogo.org/testimony/2020/01/the-state-of-whistleblower-protections-and-ideas-for-reform.

Eric Kohn, "Reality Winner Was Vilified by the American Government. This Infuriating Doc Proves She Deserved Better," IndieWire. March 17, 2021. https://www.indiewire.com/2021/03/united-states-vs-reality-winner-review-1234624223/.

Bill McCarthy, "What the Whistleblower Law Says About Sharing Complaints with Congress," Politifact, September 25, 2019. https://www.politifact.com/article/2019/sep/25/what-whistleblower-law-says-about-sharing-complain/.

Sofiia Merzlikina, "Who Are They: Whistleblowers or Spies? The US Espionage Act" Ethicontrol, February 12, 2020. https://ethicontrol.com/en/blog/espionage-usa.

Mireya Navarro, "FBI Whistleblower and Brennan Fellow Michael German Advocates for Stronger Protections So That More Whistleblowers 'Do the Right Thing,'" Brennan Center for Justice. October 8, 2019. https://www.brennancenter.org/our-work/analysis-opinion/whistleblower-explains-pitfalls-reporting-government-wrongdoing.

Nick Schwellenbach, "The Modern Politics of American Whistleblowing," Society of Professional Journalists, n.d. https://www.spj.org/whistleblower/the-modern-politics-of-american-whistleblowing.asp.

Catherine Taylor, "Freedom of the Whistleblowers: Why Prosecuting Government Leakers Under the Espionage Act Raises First Amendment Concerns." *NLG Review*, n.d. https://www.nlg.org/nlg-review/article/freedom-of-the-whistleblowers-why-prosecuting-government-leakers-under-the-espionage-act-raises-first-amendment-concerns/.

Stephen Vladeck, "Why the Whistle-Blowing Process Is Breaking Down," the *New York Times*, September 20, 2019. https://www.nytimes.com/2019/09/20/opinion/trump-whistle-blower.html.

For Further Discussion

Chapter 1

1. After reading the viewpoints in this chapter, what factors do you think determine whether a whistleblower's efforts are a success or a failure?
2. Why do you think attorneys for potential whistleblowers stress the idea of anonymity so strongly?
3. What is the practical difference between labelling people "whistleblowers" versus calling them "leakers?"

Chapter 2

1. After reading the viewpoints in this chapter, what is your opinion on rewarding whistleblowers? Are rewards too high?
2. In your opinion, are the rewards whistleblowers stand to gain worth the harassment, career jeopardy, and other troubles they are likely to endure? Explain your answer.
3. If whistleblowers were not rewarded, do you think anyone would engage in whistleblowing activity? Why or why not?

Chapter 3

1. After reading the viewpoints in this chapter, do you believe the police should be "defunded" or reformed in some major fashion?
2. After reading the viewpoints in this chapter, what do you think about "qualified immunity," which protects police officers who have committed wrongdoing from personal lawsuits?
3. In Larry Casey's viewpoint, he states that the police code of silence is mostly "an honorable one compared to all other professions." Do you agree or disagree? Explain your answer.

Chapter 4

1. After reading the viewpoints in this chapter, what is your opinion about using the Espionage Act as a way to prosecute government whistleblowers?
2. What is your opinion on whistleblowers Edward Snowden and Reality Winner? Are they heroes or traitors? Explain your reasoning.
3. After reading the viewpoints in this chapter, why do you think the Bush, Obama, and Trump administrations have been so hard on government whistleblowers as opposed to previous regimes?

Organizations to Contact

The editors have compiled the following list of organizations concerned with the issues debated in this book. The descriptions are derived from materials provided by the organizations. All have publications or information available for interested readers. The list was compiled on the date of publication of the present volume; the information provided here may change. Be aware that many organizations take several weeks or longer to respond to inquiries, so allow as much time as possible.

Empower Oversight: Whistleblowers & Research (EMPOWR)

601 King Street, Suite 200
Alexandria, VA 22314
website: https://empowr.us/

Empower Oversight Whistleblowers & Research (EMPOWR) is a nonprofit, nonpartisan educational organization dedicated to enhancing independent oversight of government and corporate wrongdoing. EMPOWR works to help insiders document and report corruption to the proper authorities while also seeking to hold authorities accountable to act on those reports. With decades of experience conducting congressional investigations that exposed major scandals and experts who wrote the laws on modern-day whistleblower protections, EMPOWR is well-positioned to combat waste, fraud, and abuse both inside and outside government.

The National Whistleblower Center (NWC)

3238 P Street NW,
Washington DC 20007
(202) 457-0034
email: info@whistleblowers.org
website: www.whistleblowers.org

The National Whistleblower Center (NWC) is a nonprofit dedicated to protecting and rewarding whistleblowers around the world. They assist whistleblowers in finding legal aid, advocate for stronger whistleblower protection laws, and educate the public about whistleblowers' critical role in protecting democracy and the rule of law. Educating whistleblowers is a top priority of the National Whistleblower Center. NWC helps whistleblowers exercise their rights by providing education and training through workshops, reports, and regular postings to their website, blog, email list, and social media channels.

Project on Government Oversight (POGO)

1100 13th Street NW, Suite 800
Washington, DC 20005
(202) 347-1122
email: info@pogo.org
website: www.pogo.org

The Project on Government Oversight (POGO) is a nonpartisan independent watchdog organization that investigates and exposes waste, corruption, and abuse of power. They become involved when government fails to serve the public or silences those who report wrongdoing. They champion reforms to achieve a more effective, ethical, and accountable federal government that safeguards constitutional principles.

Public Employees for Environmental Responsibility (PEER)

962 Wayne Ave, Suite 610
Silver Spring, MD 20910
(202) 265-7337
email: info@peer.org
website: https://peer.org/

Public Employees for Environmental Responsibility (PEER) supports current and former public employees who seek a higher standard of environmental ethics and scientific integrity within their agencies. They do this by defending whistleblowers, shining a light on improper or illegal government actions, working to improve laws and regulations, and supporting the work of other organizations. All of their services are provided pro bono, without charge. Through PEER, public servants can choose to work as "anonymous activists" so that public agencies must confront the message, rather than the messenger.

The Signals Network

268 Bush Street
#4216
San Francisco, CA 94104
email: info@thesignalsnetwork.org
website: https://thesignalsnetwork.org/

The Signals Network supports whistleblowers and helps coordinate international media investigations that speak out against corporate misconduct and human rights abuses. They provide customized support services to a selected number of whistleblowers who have contributed to published reports of significant wrongdoing. They also empower workers and whistleblowers by educating them about their right to report wrongdoing and speak out.

Whistleblower Aid

email: press@whistlebloweraid.org.
website: https://whistlebloweraid.org/

Whistleblower Aid is a nonprofit legal organization in Washington, DC. They support individuals who lawfully report government and corporate law breaking. They can provide assistance to individuals in the United States or abroad who want to disclose illegal conduct, including misconduct relating to: the United States government or federal officials; securities fraud by corporate officers, investment advisors, or stock brokers; foreign governments or their representatives; local or state governments, including police and prosecutors; violations of the tax, labor, or environmental laws; sexual violence or harassment; and organized crime, human trafficking, and mass atrocities.

The Whistleblower and Source Protection Program (WHISPeR) at ExposeFacts

1717 K Street, NW, Suite 900
Washington, DC 20006
email: whisper@exposefacts.org
website: https://whisper.exposefacts.org/

The Whistleblower and Source Protection Program (WHISPeR) at ExposeFacts facilitates investigative journalism in the public interest by providing pro bono, direct legal representation to whistleblowers and media sources with a focus on human rights and civil liberties. WHISPeR gives clients the support they need to bring transparency to otherwise unaccountable national security agencies and programs. WHISPeR's work encompasses impact litigation, media outreach, and policy advocacy. WHISPeR unlocks information in the public interest, fosters high-quality investigative journalism, protects the freedoms of speech and the press, and furthers the most critical component of a democratic society: an informed citizenry.

Whistleblowers of America (WoA)

11130 Lillian Highway
Pensacola, FL 32506
(202) 643-1956
email: Info@whistleblowersofamerica.org
website: www.whistleblowersofamerica.org

Whistleblowers of America (WoA) is a nonprofit organization aiding whistleblowers who have suffered retaliation after having identified harm to individuals or the public. Whistleblowers of America provides education and training, peer to peer support, and mediation services. WoA engages the media in a public advocacy campaign on behalf of whistleblowers and watchdogs.

Bibliography of Books

Tatiana Bazzichelli. *Whistleblowing for Change: Exposing Systems of Power and Injustice.* Bielefeld, Germany: Transcript Verlag, 2021.

Martin Bright. *Whistleblowers: The Lifeblood of Democracy.* Los Angeles, CA: Sage, 2021.

Susan J. Fowler. *Whistleblower: My Journey to Silicon Valley and Fight for Justice at Uber.* New York, NY: Viking, 2020.

Ryan Hartwig and Kent Heckenlively. *Behind the Mask of Facebook: A Whistleblower's Shocking Story of Big Tech Bias and Censorship.* New York, NY: Skyhorse Publishing, 2021.

Sanja Kutnjak Ivković, Jon Maskály, Ahmet Kule, Maria Maki Haberfeld, eds. *Police Code of Silence in Times of Change.* New York, NY: Springer, 2022.

Anna E. Lindner, ed. *Whistleblowers* (Current Controversies). New York, NY: Greenhaven Publishing, 2020.

New York Times Editorial Staff. *Whistleblowers: Chelsea Manning, Edward Snowden and Others* (Public Profiles). New York, NY: New York Times Educational Publishing, 2019.

Arnold Jason Ross. *Whistleblowers Leakers and Their Networks: From Snowden to Samizdat.* MD: Rowman & Littlefield, 2020.

Robert Samuels and Toluse Olorunnipa. *His Name Is George Floyd: One Man's Life and the Struggle for Racial Justice.* New York, NY: Viking, 2022.

Edward J. Snowden. *Permanent Record: How One Man Exposed the Truth About Government Spying and Digital Security.* New York, NY: Henry Holt and Company, 2021.

Index